The Ordinances
Teach Us
to Be Baptists

The Ordinances
Teach Us
to Be Baptists

The Ordinances Display the Gospel
& Define Baptist Polity and Practice

Marty Marriott

Maranatha Baptist University Press
745 West Main Street
Watertown, WI 53094

Editor: Rebecca Brock
Cover Graphic Artist: Matthew Holloway
Proofreader, Typesetter: Denise Graziano

Cover photo is of Pastor Joshua Roberts baptizing a convert in the historic Penuel Baptist Church in Rhosllannerchrugog, Wales, UK. Used with permission.

ISBN 978-0-9821426-7-7

CONTENTS

Preface

As a Baptist, I am convinced that a biblical understanding of the ordinances—both baptism and the Lord's Supper—is paramount. Sadly, after decades of ministry, I'm also convinced that our local churches are unknowingly, largely ignorant on the issue. I have frequently asked candidates during ordination councils about the purpose, order, and frequency of each ordinance. I have found the candidates, though educated in Baptist colleges and seminaries, easily stumped by the simplest of questions, and some even surprised by the line of questioning.

As you read this book, I trust you will discover the importance of the ordinances to a clear practice and presentation of the New Testament faith. I have attempted to be understandable and biblical. I have done nothing to make the reading more difficult or to elevate the discussion to seem more scholarly. Every believer can grasp the scriptural principles associated with the ordinances. This book is intended for *you*—to read, to understand, and to practice.

You may find this book somewhat repetitious, but hopefully not boringly redundant. The repetition is by design to provide the necessary foundation in the immediate context. At the same time, the book is not intended to be comprehensive in dealing with every passage of Scripture referring to the ordinances. I trust you will see that the teaching of all other Scriptures is consistent with the principles presented here.

I pray this book will bring clarity to the importance of baptism and the Lord's Supper. When we embrace these truths afresh, it will strengthen our churches in immeasurable ways.

Dr. Marty Marriott
Chancellor
Maranatha Baptist University

Introduction

The two ordinances themselves, both baptism and the Lord's Supper, *teach* believers about the person and work of Christ and the nature of the local church—its composition, purpose, and function. The following chapters will support this proposition by focusing on the meaning of the ordinances in relation to New Testament truth about Christ (Christology) and His church (Ecclesiology).

Chapters 1-2 seek to answer the basic question, "What is an ordinance?" After distinguishing a biblical ordinance from a Catholic or Reformed sacrament, we will examine the three characteristics of a biblical ordinance.

Chapters 3-5 consider the relationship of the ordinances to Christ and to the local church. Chapter 3 ends with a vital consideration of John 6, a passage distorted by the Roman Catholic Church and misunderstood by many Christians. This critical passage has far-reaching implications for the meaning and practice of the Lord's Supper. Chapter 4 explains the meaning and purpose of baptism, refuting both infant baptism and baptismal regeneration. The chapter concludes by discussing both the valid authority and proper administrator of the ordinance. Chapter 5 concentrates on the Lord's Supper as a church ordinance, focusing particularly on Paul's writing to the church at Corinth in 1 Corinthians 11. We will also examine open, closed, and close communion practices.

Chapter 6 points out that the ordinances define church membership, direct local church practice, and contribute to the harmonious relationship of all the Baptist distinctives. While "there is nothing new under the sun," I trust to demonstrate the harmony of Baptist beliefs in a manner I have not seen discussed elsewhere.

An often-overlooked teaching in the last several generations is the relationship of the ordinances to each other. Chapter 7 deals with their distinct meaning, as well as the frequency and order of observance. These truths have great implications for the local church.

Chapter 8 deals with the most important distinctive of a Baptist church: regenerate, immersed church membership. We will contrast this distinctive with the practices of various denominations and demonstrate that Baptist practice conforms to New Testament teaching.

The book concludes with a question and answer section, containing concise statements of the book's conclusions.

My prayerful hope is that the Spirit will use the truth unfolded in this small volume to enlighten you for Christian growth and invigorate you for service in the local church.

1

What is an Ordinance? (Part 1)

Both Protestant and Reformed churches put great emphasis on baptism and the Lord's Supper, calling them *sacraments*. But the two ordinances are not sacraments; they offer no saving grace in themselves. Rather, the ordinances are divinely ordained pictures, illustrations, or memorials. They teach us by illustration. Both ordinances picture 1) the truth of the person and work of Christ and 2) the application of those truths to the Christian life and church ministry. Some Baptists have erroneously adopted the language of two "sacraments" because of the historical Reformation roots of many English Baptists. As we shall see, however, this terminology should be rejected.

For centuries, Roman Catholics have referred to "church sacraments." Historians and theologians have noted that Roman Catholicism was built around two falsehoods: sacerdotalism and sacramentalism. The former attributes supernatural powers to the priesthood; the latter teaches that religious rites are channels of grace necessary for salvation. Baptists repudiate both teachings. When properly understood and practiced, the ordinances properly identify authentic Baptist churches.

Baptist professor and historian, Dr. Richard Weeks, first introduced me to the significance of the ordinances. In his Baptist Polity class in 1974, he described the differences between a symbol, a rite, and an ordinance:

- A *symbol* is a sign or visible representation of an invisible truth or idea.
- A *rite* is a symbol which is employed with regularity and sacred intent.
- An *ordinance* is a symbolic rite which sets forth the central truths of the Christian faith along with its universal and perpetual obligations.

The ordinances teach us; they were designed and given for that purpose.

The ordinances predate the church.

Baptism and the Lord's Supper predate the birth and organization of the church. Whatever else it may have meant, John's baptism was certainly anticipatory of the work of Christ. Likewise, the baptisms performed by the apostles and recorded in the Gospels were prophetic of the death, burial, and resurrection of Jesus Christ.

The Lord's Supper was clearly anticipatory of the Lord's death on the cross. When, prior to His death, He commanded His disciples, "This do in remembrance of me," the Lord Jesus was introducing the apostles to His work on Calvary. Through the Supper He prophetically spoke of giving His flesh and shedding His blood. It is because of what Christ did on the cross that disciples are made, then baptized, and taught all the commands of Jesus. These ordinances both predate and anticipate the church.

The ordinances predate the completion of Scripture.

Baptism and the Lord's Supper were designed to instruct us. The early church did not have the completed Scriptures. The writings of the apostles were copied, circulated, and publicly read in the various churches. These copies were extremely rare. Paul explicitly states that he intended the book of Colossians to be circulated to other churches.

> *(Colossians 4:16) And when this epistle is read among you, cause that it be read also in the church of the Laodiceans; and that ye likewise read the epistle from Laodicea.*

Such was the case with the letters to the seven churches and with the entire book of Revelation.

> *(Revelation 1:3) Blessed is he that **readeth**, and they that **hear** the words of this prophecy, and keep those things which are written therein: for the time is at hand.*

> *(Revelation 22:17) And the Spirit and the bride say, Come. And let him that **heareth** say, Come. And let him that is athirst come. And whosoever will, let him take the water of life freely.*

From the church's first gatherings, the ordinances were introduced as necessary and repeatable practices. While celebrating the ordinances, the early church displayed the gospel to one another and gave direction regarding church order. However, this symbolism was not provision for autonomous and unusual interpretations, because the apostles had the leadership of the Holy Spirit and the authority of God. As the epistles were written, the unfolding truth was consistent with the truth already being displayed through the ordinances.

In this way, the apostles were *teaching* soteriology and ecclesiology prior to the completion of the canon of truth. The ordinances would provide both the foundation and the support for their instruction.

In defending the mode of baptism and the meaning of the Lord's Supper, and referring to the ritual nature of the ordinances, Henry Colby observed,

> The spiritual is more important than the ritual, but why was the ritual appointed? Was it not in order the better to conserve and uphold the spiritual? Was it not admirably shaped and adapted

to that end? If the Lord has thus given us the ritual, a beautiful vase, as it were, wherein we may more easily keep and guard the heavenly treasure of the spiritual, *let us see to it that the vase becomes neither broken nor distorted, nor turned upside down!* If Christians have thought it worth while to spare no pains, in order to obtain the language of the original Scriptures, even to the order of the words, because that language is the permanent expression of spiritual truth; *certainly it is incumbent upon us to guard with the most sedulous [diligent] care the exact form and order of those New Testament ordinances, which the Lord intended to be so deeply significant*[1] (emphasis added).

The late Pastor W. A. Criswell spoke to the importance of the ordinances in proclaiming the gospel:

> In the wisdom—in the infinite wisdom of Christ, the Lord took the common experiences of all men everywhere, and He placed in those common human experiences the tremendously meaningful, foundational, fundamental truths of the gospel. All men everywhere eat and drink. All men everywhere know death and burial. And the Lord took those common, universal human experiences, and He sealed in them the great truths of the gospel.
>
> The ordinances are a dramatization to the eye of the great truth of the gospel. They do not procure our salvation, they proclaim it. They do not possess magic; they witness to a majestic truth. They do not expiate our sins; they exhibit the atoning love and grace of our Lord. They proclaim the gospel message. They are memorials; they are done in remembrance. These are tremendous monuments that we could never, ever forget, to what Christ has done for us. They are visible; they are

---

[1] Henry Colby, *Restriction of the Lord's Supper* (Watertown, WI: Roger Williams Heritage Archives, 1853), 34.

effective; they are glorious.[2]

A person painting a portrait reproduces the likeness of the subject as closely as possible so that those viewing it in the coming decades and centuries will have an accurate representation of the subject painted. In the same way, the ordinances were designed by our God to represent, and so promote and protect, the foundational truths of Christianity and the church.

We are not Baptists just because we choose to practice the ordinances in a certain way; we are Baptists because of what the ordinances teach us. They give us particular and perpetual guidance on the foundational truths of Christianity as well as the organization and practice of the local church. If they are practiced correctly, the church will display pictures which accurately proclaim Christ and faithfully preserve the truth in local church polity.

Like driving on a highway, the ordinances are our road markers to keep us traveling in the right direction, and they are also the lane lines and guard rails which keep us safely on the road of New Testament truth and practice.

To protect the gospel, we need to protect the ordinances, which perpetually instruct us on the true gospel and church practice. One writer described the ordinances in relation to the gospel itself, designating the gospel as the capital city and the ordinances as the suburbs:

> By God's grace the center is increasingly secure, but the center isn't all there is. And if we make the center everything and everything else nothing, we set ourselves up to lose the center itself.[3]

---

[2] W. A. Criswell Sermon Library. "The Ordinances of the Church." http://wacriswell.com.

[3] Bobby Jamieson. *Going Public: Why Baptism Is Required for Church Membership* (Nashville, TN: B&H Academic 2015, eBook), 12.

To protect the capital, we must protect the suburbs. To protect the gospel, we must unashamedly protect the ordinances. Many critical voices are attacking those who protest the distortion of the ordinances, crying out that the gospel is what is important and not the pictures of the gospel. Their seemingly noble and loving affirmations of the central truth of the gospel are at the expense of those "suburbs" which protect the gospel. The distortion of the ordinances has led to a lack of gospel clarity and too often to an undermining of the gospel itself, as well as the corruption of both the purpose and order of the local church.

The ordinances, correctly practiced, protect the gospel and the order and polity of the church which Jesus loves.

The ordinances have three common characteristics.

The two ordinances exhibit three characteristics in the New Testament:

- Each was *commanded by Christ.*
- Each was *practiced by the early church.*
- Each is *explained* or *expounded in the epistles.*

Some groups claim foot-washing is an ordinance, but only baptism and the Lord's Supper meet these three standards. Foot-washing does not qualify because it was neither universally practiced in the early churches of Christ, nor was its meaning expounded in the epistles. Though the book of Acts records the practice of both baptism and the Lord's Supper, there is no record of foot-washing being observed in any church.

Others claim there are even more commands or ordinances for the church to follow. However, other practices or commands (1 Cor. 11:2) do not rise to the same level of importance; they do not have the same unique purpose. Baptism and the Lord's Supper have a foundational purpose that gives them a unique place in the church. Only these two are pictures of the past, present, and future work of salvation. The reason Baptists speak of only two ordinances is because these are the only practices commanded by the Lord Jesus that symbolize the substitutionary atonement of Christ, and both are exclusively practiced in relation to the church. The commands to pray, to preach and teach, to publicly read Scripture, to use our spiritual gifts, to minister to one another in various ways, and to sing are distinct from the two ordinances in this regard, because none of these are exclusive to the gathered local church.

The New Testament teaches that baptism and the Lord's Supper are both a memorial and a prophecy. Each looks back to the finished work of Christ on the cross, and each possesses a future aspect as well. The Lord's Supper is celebrated until Christ comes, while baptism anticipates the future resurrection of all believers.

These three characteristics—commanded by Christ, practiced in the early churches, and explained in the New Testament epistles—limit our consideration of the ordinances to baptism and the Lord's Supper. We will consider these characteristics in detail in later chapters.

2

What is an Ordinance? (Part 2)

We have seen several truths about an ordinance: it follows conversion, is not a sacrament, and confers no grace to the recipient. An ordinance neither provides nor produces personal salvation but is a picture of the salvation provided in Christ. The distinguishing characteristics of an ordinance are clear: it is commanded by Christ, practiced in the early church, and its meaning is explained primarily in the New Testament epistles. Let's consider each.

They are commanded by Christ.

It is true that Jesus did not baptize any of His followers. His disciples were baptized by John and the twelve baptized others.

> *(John 4:1-2) When therefore the Lord knew how the Pharisees had heard that Jesus made and baptized more disciples than John, [2](Though Jesus himself baptized not, but his disciples,)*

This is not to say that the Lord was uninterested or indifferent to water baptism. John was the prophesied forerunner of Christ and as such, he was fulfilling the Lord's will. Further evidence of the importance and necessity of baptism is revealed in the Savior's own baptism. This baptism, in the Lord's words, was "to fulfill all righteousness" (Matt. 3:15). Jesus Christ's baptism was not a testimony of His own redemption, as it is with all believers in Him, but a prophetic declaration of what He would do for us in His death, burial, and resurrection. His baptism was witnessed by the descending of the Holy Spirit and the words of the Father declaring Him to be His own beloved Son (Matt. 3:17). And so, in His baptism we see the proclaiming of his deity and picturing of His victorious work of redemption. Before his ascension our Lord commanded the baptizing of disciples until the end of the age (Matt. 28:18-20).

The historical context for understanding the Lord's Supper

On the night before His death, our Lord Jesus Christ gathered with His disciples in the upper room to eat the Passover meal. Every year the Jewish people celebrated the Passover as a special meal designed by God to remember the deliverance of Israel from Egypt.

As prophesied to Abraham, Israel suffered bondage in Egypt. After 400 years, God delivered them from Egypt and led them into the land of Canaan. In doing so, God brought upon Egypt and Pharaoh a series of plagues. After the tenth plague, which was the death of every firstborn throughout the entire land of Egypt, Pharaoh finally let the children of Israel depart.

The children of Israel's firstborn were "passed over" or protected from the death angel by applying the blood of a lamb to the doorposts and lintels of their dwellings. Since then, whenever an Israelite participated in the annual Passover feast, he would remember that God delivered his nation out of Egyptian bondage.

Jesus transformed the Passover when He instructed His disciples to drink of the cup and eat of the bread in remembrance of His death for them. Calvary was the ultimate fulfillment of the Passover celebration where Messiah Jesus gave His life for the sins of all humanity. Christ's work on the cross provided redemption through His blood for all who have faith in Him. The cross of Christ has superseded the exodus from Egypt as the greatest redemptive event in history. Christians remember the blood shed at the cross.

(Colossians 1:13-14) Who hath delivered us from the power of darkness, and hath translated us into the kingdom of his dear Son: [14]In whom we have redemption through his blood, even the forgiveness of sins:

As the Lamb of God, Jesus was the fulfillment of the Passover sacrifice.

(John 1:29) The next day John seeth Jesus coming unto him, and saith, Behold the Lamb of God, which taketh away the sin of the world.

(1 Corinthians 5:7) Purge out therefore the old leaven, that ye may be a new lump, as ye are unleavened. For even Christ our passover is sacrificed for us:

In this context, the Lord's Supper is a memorial instituted by Jesus Christ Himself. He provided deliverance from sin and death when He died on the cross and shed His blood.

The biblical references to Christ's commands

Baptism was commanded by Jesus Christ in His final message to His apostles (Matthew 28:18-20). Baptizing was to be integral to the disciple-making endeavors of the apostles and to the local churches to follow. On Pentecost, Peter commanded repentance and water baptism in the name of Jesus Christ (Acts 2:38).

The Lord's Supper was also commanded by Christ (Matt. 26:26-29; Mk. 14:22-25; Lk. 22:14-20; I Cor. 11:23-34). The command of the Lord is repeated in all three synoptic Gospels and in Paul's letter to the Corinthians. John speaks of the occasion and gives additional details focusing on Judas and the night of betrayal.

The Lord's instruction to the Corinthian church includes the commands, "Take eat" (11:24) and "This do" (11:24,25). Let's consider the instructions for celebrating the Lord's Supper as found in 1 Corinthians 11.

(1 Corinthians 11:23) For I have received of the Lord that which also I delivered unto you...

What Paul said to the Corinthian church was not his own opinion; he received the instructions from the Lord. It wasn't some tradition that had been handed down from person to person, but rather, it was revelation directly from the Lord Jesus. Therefore, Paul's instructions concerning the Lord's Supper are not merely his suggestions, but they are the Lord's commands. This makes the Lord's Supper not just something we could do or should do; the Lord's Supper is a ***must do*** for the local church. We are commanded to observe the Lord's Supper. It is one of the two ordinances that Jesus gave to be perpetuated in the church.

And so, Jesus commanded that all believers observe these ordinances, but not as a means of grace or as a sacrament. Baptism was observed "because of" or "with reference to" forgiveness of sins (Acts 2:38). Baptism followed repentance and faith as a testimony of conversion.

As we have noted, sacramental teaching says that these and other rites are a physical means by which men obtain grace from God. This teaching is rooted in Roman Catholic doctrine and currently perpetuated through Covenant or Reformed Theology which practices pedobaptism (infant baptism). Covenantalists, who baptize or sprinkle babies, often reason that "regeneration can take place in the smallest of infants... in the sphere of the covenant of God. He usually regenerates His elect children from infancy."[4]

Sacramentalists agree with covenantalists that baptism brings infants into the church and is the sign of the covenant. One of the main reasons that Anabaptists were severely and persistently persecuted, and some martyred, by both Catholics and Protestants was because they rejected infant baptism as the conferring of grace through an outward act. However, the

---

[4] Herman Hoeksema, *Reformed Dogmatics* (Jenison, MI: Reformed Free Publishing Association, 1966), 464.

Anabaptist's persecutors believed in Augustine's baptism of infants with its "magical" powers of regeneration, which provided access into the church and to God.

Because the ordinances were commanded by Christ, and since both the Catholic and Reformed think they are necessary for regeneration and forgiveness of sins, it is not surprising that church-state governments demanded infant baptism and condemned believer's baptism. Calvin wrote, "God in baptism promises remission of sins, and will undoubtedly perform what he has promised to all believers. That promise was offered to us in baptism, let us therefore embrace it in faith."[5] Augustine, the hero of John Calvin, supported the death penalty for those who were rebaptized as believers after conversion to Christ.[6]

The terminology used in both Catholic and Protestant churches can be very misleading. They often speak of faith and affirm the truth of salvation by grace but say nothing about how that grace is received. Is it imparted mystically by a sacrament or imputed by faith alone in Christ's finished work? The Bible teaching is clear that grace comes by faith alone (Eph. 2:8-9).

In a symbolic view of baptism and the Lord's Supper, Baptist practices are distinctly different from all those in Reformed, Protestant church traditions. This is because we differ sharply in our doctrinal beliefs. The ordinances, properly understood and observed, support the truths of Christ and the church. And the antithesis is equally true. The gospel, properly understood and preached, leads to a symbolic view of the ordinances for believers in the churches.

---

[5] James White, *The Potter's Freedom* (Amityville, NY: Calvary Press Publishing, 2000), 101.

[6] He used a distorted view of Luke 14:23 to compel those who are involved in heresies and schisms to come into line with Rome. This same thinking was embraced by Calvin. Dave Hunt, What Love Is This? Calvinism's Misrepresentation of God (Bend, OR: Berean Call, 2007), 47.

They are practiced in the local churches.

The record of the practice

The baptism of converts is part of the Great Commission, and clearly the practice of the apostles and those who followed them. There is almost no disagreement that baptism was commanded by Jesus to be practiced in the church until the end of the age (Matthew 28:18-20; Acts 2:41). Only unbelievers and hyper-dispensationalists have disputed this truth.

The Lord's Supper is to be practiced in the local churches (Acts 2:42; 20:7; 1 Cor. 11:17f). The repeated phrase in 1 Corinthians 11, "come together," clearly prescribes the ordinance is to be observed in the corporate church setting when its members assemble (11:17,18,20,33,34). This is a local church ordinance and is not properly observed in other venues.

> *(1 Corinthians 11:33-34) Wherefore, my brethren, **when ye come together** to eat, tarry one for another. 34 And if any man hunger, let him eat at home; that ye **come** not **together** unto condemnation. And the rest will I set in order when I come.*

The requirements for participation

The requirements for participation in the ordinances are not first determined by the church through its officers. To be sure, the church is responsible for guarding the proper administration of the ordinances, but the requirements are decided at a much higher level. God gives them in the pages of the New Testament.

1) Baptism is for those who have exercised faith in Christ.

Baptism is reserved for those capable of intelligent faith and therefore, not to be performed on infants. Only those who have believed the gospel, and are thereby born again, are the proper candidates.

As we can easily learn from the Book of Acts, baptism was performed on all, without exception, who believed in Jesus

Christ. Faith was always the condition precedent for baptism.[7]

Through personal faith in Christ Jesus, and not baptism, God regards the believer as crucified, dead, buried, raised, and united with Christ to live perpetually for Himself. This has been the understanding of conversion from apostolic times.

   2) *The Lord's Supper is for those who have been scripturally baptized.*

The New Testament gives clear terms for participation at the Lord's Table:

Regeneration. Only saved people are to participate in the Lord's Supper. Since the New Testament teaches regenerate church membership (see chapter 8), and since the Lord's Supper is a local church ordinance, only saved people should participate in the communion service.

Baptism.[8] The practice of the early church established the order. Converts were baptized upon their profession of faith and then continued in the routine of church life, which included preaching, fellowship, the breaking of bread, and prayer (Acts 2:41-42).

Obedience. Since baptism is a profession of becoming a disciple of Christ (Matt. 28:19), it is unthinkable that one who is truly converted would continue on a path of disobedience to God. Therefore, it would be improper to baptize one who has no intention or desire to follow Christ's commands.

As believers, we are exhorted to examine ourselves prior to partaking of the Lord's Supper (1 Cor. 11:28). It is impossible for any believer to live perfectly, but it is expected that each one would live submissively. Those who are living with unconfessed sin or who are set in the path of willful disobedience, ought to refrain from the Supper. To these individuals, the Lord's Supper becomes a call to repentance and renewed commitment to

---

[7] Johannes Warns, *Baptism*, trans G. H. Lang (London: The Paternoster Press, 1957), 25.
[8] Only immersion is baptism.

obedience. Then, the picture in the ordinance becomes a true representation of the fellowship between the believer and Christ.

They are explained in the New Testament.

Baptism

Baptism declares that the believer is a follower of Jesus Christ. It is a public confession of his faith in, and commitment to, Jesus Christ. Water baptism is a practical demonstration of a spiritual reality which has already taken place in the life of a repentant believer.

At salvation the old man is buried and forgotten; the new man is empowered by Christ to walk in newness of life. This new walk is enablement for a new direction, a new conduct, and a new destination. Through baptism it is as if the new convert is saying, "The old life is dead. There's no hope for the old life; it is gone."

Yet this is far from the common understanding. The truth is often distorted or denied. For example, the Christian Reformed Church has a sermon posted on their denominational website to communicate their position on baptism, particularly the baptism of infants:

> To understand our position more fully on infant baptism, we offer this text of a sermon, from January 13, 2002, by Rev. David Feddes, former English radio minister with Back to God Ministries International (now ReFrame Ministries).[9]

Feddes begins with a plea for unity, in effect diminishing the New Testament's mode and purpose of baptism. Feddes indicates that individuals and churches have differing views that are equally valid, but then goes on to champion his own view as correct.

He asserts that Christian Reformed teaching denies any saving merit to infant baptism and states emphatically that "...baptismal

---

[9] David Feddes, "Should Babies Be Baptized?" accessed January 10, 2024, https://www.crcna.org/welcome/beliefs/position-statements/baptism/should-babies-be-baptized.

regeneration, is not biblical...millions of Christians believe in infant baptism without believing in baptismal regeneration at all."[10]

But regardless of what Feddes claims, infant baptism is a perversion of the ordinance, leading to a miscommunication of the gospel and the nature of the church. The church is to be made up of regenerate members only. The church is distinct from Israel and not a covenant community or political entity.[11] The reality of this miscommunication is observed in Feddes's need to disassociate from those who teach that regeneration takes place through infant baptism and that faith then is actually "confirmed" at a later time (see chapter 8).

It's also hard to harmonize a denial of the baptismal regeneration of infants with Feddes's other assertions. He states, "All true Christians see baptism as a sign of sins being washed away and of being united with Christ's death and resurrection." Yet, these are blessings reserved for the regenerate believers and could never be true of infants unless conferred by baptism itself. Note that Feddes seems to recognize the symbolic nature of baptism but errs in ascribing it to entering a "community," described very much like a believer's entrance into the church through personal faith in Christ. He argues unconvincingly:

> Baptism is a sign and seal of entering the community of Christ, the community bought with Jesus' blood and given life by his Holy Spirit. What's the status of babies born to Christian families? Do they belong to that covenant community? Do they have a place in God's family? Are they citizens of God's kingdom?[12]

Baptists would answer these rhetorical questions with an adamant, soul-deep "No!" Unregenerate, sprinkled infants are not in the kingdom. A person must be born again (John 3:3-5).

---

[10] Feddes, "Should Babies Be Baptized?"
[11] Before you dismiss the latter as being an extreme criticism, consider that infant baptism has historically been demanded by state churches.
[12] Feddes, "Should Babies Be Baptized?"

Furthermore, they are not even in the "community of Christ"—whatever that means—because they neither have been bought with His blood nor have been given life through the Holy Spirit.

To make the Christian Reformed position[13] even more confusing, Feddes asserts:

> Even those who support infant baptism still insist that those who are baptized as babies must later respond with a public profession of personal faith in Christ as Lord and Savior, and must live for him.[14]

This statement renders infant baptism, at best, meaningless. However, infant baptism isn't valueless or meaningless; infant baptism is gravely dangerous. It is not neutral because it is communicating a different gospel. Infant baptism does not picture a point-in-time conversion through personal faith in the declared truth of the gospel. Even if there is a denial or verbal disclaimer that infant baptism confers regeneration, it is pictorially proclaiming otherwise. It is communicating that a person can become a Christian 1) through connection with a community, and 2) through an external ritual. In fact, pedobaptism pictures salvation through ritual, even when the person is unaware and uninvolved.

What realities, then, are pictured in biblical baptism?

1) A new heart separated from sin

The following verses link circumcision with baptism. What is the relationship between circumcision and baptism in this passage? Why the reference?

> *(Colossians 2:11-13) In whom also ye are circumcised with the circumcision made without hands, in putting off the body of the sins of the flesh by the circumcision of Christ: [12]Buried with him in baptism, wherein also ye are risen with him through the faith of the operation of God, who hath raised him from the dead. [13]And*

---

[13] Along with so many other churches embracing Covenant Theology.

[14] Feddes, "Should Babies Be Baptized?"

you, being dead in your sins and the uncircumcision of your flesh, hath he quickened together with him, having forgiven you all trespasses;

Both circumcision and baptism picture separation from the old patterns of sin. But it is a leap to assume that baptism has replaced circumcision and that the church has adopted infant baptism in its place. Whatever the relationship between circumcision and baptism in these texts, the following things are true:

- The circumcision of Christ is not physical; it is not done with human hands.
- This circumcision and this baptism involve the putting away of sins.
- The circumcision of Christ was already accomplished in these believing members of the church to whom Paul is writing.
- It is by faith in the operation or working of God (Col. 2:12) that we are raised.
- This baptism deals with sin and forgiveness of offenses.
- Believers are made alive through this baptism; God having forgiven their trespasses (Col. 2:13).

The connections between baptism and circumcision seem to be in the separation from sin and the identification with Christ, having been buried with Him in baptism and raised with Him as well.

The Apostle Paul is clearly referring to Spirit baptism (1 Cor 12:13), which water baptism pictures. The baptism of the Holy Spirit takes place at the time of faith in Jesus Christ. At that moment, a believer receives forgiveness of sins and is raised with Christ to walk in newness of life (Rom. 6:3-4).

The Reformed interpretation begins with a false hermeneutic that fails to see the distinction the Scriptures make between Israel and the New Testament church. The logic below is based upon the faulty assumption that Israel has in some sense become the church. Speaking of the infant children of believers, the Reformed

Church writer, Feddes, asks,

> How, then, can the church refuse them the sign of citizenship in God's kingdom and membership in his family? God's covenant has always included not only believers but their children as well...it would be a shocking letdown if the God who included children of believers in the old era excluded them in the new era. How could babies from covenant families, circumcised in the old era, not be baptized in the new era?[15]

Paul's point was to describe a similarity between Old Testament circumcision and New Testament baptism. He did not say that the latter had replaced the former. Each, in its own way and for its intended people, had a spiritual reality that was pictured by outward observance. God called for more than physical circumcision; he commanded the people of Israel to be circumcised in heart, to repent of sin, and seek Him (Deut. 10:16; 30:6; Jer. 4:4). Spirit baptism is similar in that it involves forgiveness of sin and a new life in Christ, a life separate from the deadness of sin.

There are obvious differences in the two. Circumcision was only for male Israelites and proselytes, whereas baptism is for all believing males and females from all nations of the world. And it is at this point that the conflating of the two becomes the most problematic. If all of these blessing are pictured in circumcision, how does this relate to infants? What is the picture for them?

And so, based upon a faulty hermeneutic, the author, who fairly represents the Reformed position, once again asserts that the baptism of infants is required because they are part of the household of faith. He writes:

> The gospel addresses households, and it's biblical to respond as households. Biblical faith declares, "As for me and my household, we will serve the Lord" (Joshua 24:15). In the Old Testament, when the head of a household was circumcised, his

---

[15] Feddes, "Should Babies Be Baptized?"

boys were also circumcised. In the New Testament, when the head of a household was baptized, the rest of the household was also baptized. Today, too, churches should baptize individual converts and the children under their care.[16]

The author makes a declaration based upon a defective theology without giving any scriptural support, other than the one Old Testament reference. The sermon concludes:

To be born into a Christian family and be baptized as a baby is no substitute for personal faith; it makes the call for personal faith all the more powerful and urgent. That's why churches that baptize babies of believers also insist that when those children reach a point where they're able to make up their own minds, they must make a personal, public profession of faith in Christ.[17]

In this conclusion there is a confession of the error. The author clearly repudiates the value of infant baptism. Salvation comes by personal faith at a point when an individual can exercise intelligent faith in Christ. Church membership is for those who have personally believed the gospel and have been immersed in testimony of their conversion. Infant baptism distorts the gospel and destroys the mission of the church.

2) Death to old life

The following Scriptures refer to Holy Spirit baptism. However, water baptism pictures the spiritual reality and is instructive of what takes place through the Spirit's work.

(Colossians 2:12) Buried with him in baptism, wherein also ye are risen with him through the faith of the operation of God, who hath raised him from the dead.

(Romans 6:4) Therefore we are buried with him by baptism into death: that like as Christ was raised up from the dead by the glory

---

[16] Feddes, "Should Babies Be Baptized?"
[17] Ibid.

of the Father, even so we also should walk in newness of life.

Going under the water illustrates a burial of the believer's old life; coming up out of the water proclaims a resurrection, God raising him from the dead as He did Christ. The believing sinner once dead in sins, separated from, and incapable of knowing God, is made alive in Christ and enabled to walk in new life.

Water baptism is a way to visually preach the gospel. Baptism pictures the death, burial, and resurrection of Christ, and our identification with Him in each of these. Christ's work paid the penalty of our sins. By faith in Him, we bury the old life, and we rise to walk in a new life. "Once 'out of Christ' now 'in Christ,' made one with Him: this it is which testified through baptism."[18]

3) Newness of life

Baptism is a testimony that, through faith in the saving work of Jesus Christ, a believer has died to the old life, and the values of the old world, and is now living a new life for things of eternity. Being born again means to become a new creation (2 Cor. 5:17) or to be regenerated by God's Spirit.

> *(John 3:3-5) Jesus answered and said unto him, Verily, verily, I say unto thee, Except a man be born again, he cannot see the kingdom of God. ⁴Nicodemus saith unto him, How can a man be born when he is old? can he enter the second time into his mother's womb, and be born? ⁵Jesus answered, Verily, verily, I say unto thee, Except a man be born of water and of the Spirit, he cannot enter into the kingdom of God.*

When the believer is raised to walk in newness of life (Rom. 6:4), he enters a brand new world. He now sees the world with spiritual eyes of understanding. When Paul says that he knows no man after the flesh (2 Cor. 5:16), he is speaking of a new perspective on others; he now sees every individual as a person for whom Christ died. He is now seeing the world through the eyes of Christ and the truth of God. Prior to receiving this new life,

---

[18] Warns, *Baptism*, 29.

unbelievers thought on earthly things (Phil 2). Thinking on heavenly things is not only possible but a normal expectation of the Christian (Col 3:2).

In the Book of Revelation, the unconverted are repeatedly called "them that dwell upon the earth" or earth dwellers (Rev. 6:10; 11:10; 13:14; 14:6; 17:8). This is not a mere geographical designation; this speaks of their spiritual orientation. Their hearts are set on the temporal and the physical rather than the values of the eternal God.

4) A new identity

This new life involves a new identity. Being in Christ now becomes our primary identity.

> *(Galatians 3:27) For as many of you as have been baptized into Christ have put on Christ.*

We do not cease to be male or female, Jew or Gentile, or even slave or free. Our biological, ethnic, and social standing is unchanged, but these are secondary descriptors to that of being identified as Christians with equal access to God through His Son.

A new identity involves wearing a new uniform of Christlikeness. We are now representatives of God through Christ. This is an identity vastly more important than anything physical, ethnic, or social.

5) Cleansing

> *(Acts 22:16) And now why tarriest thou? arise, and be baptized, and wash away thy sins, calling on the name of the Lord.*

Some have mistakenly sought support in this verse for baptismal regeneration. Obviously, Paul did not understand Ananias's words to mean that baptism saves. Paul knew he was converted before Ananias spoke to him. These words, when properly understood in the broader context of Scripture, are in full agreement with the New Testament teaching that salvation is by faith alone.

Paul himself clarified this when he wrote to the Romans.

(Romans 10:8-10) But what saith it? The word is nigh thee, even in thy mouth, and in thy heart: that is, the word of faith, which we preach; 9 That if thou shalt confess with thy mouth the Lord Jesus, and shalt believe in thine heart that God hath raised him from the dead, thou shalt be saved. 10 For with the heart man believeth unto righteousness; and with the mouth confession is made unto salvation.

Baptism is an open confession of one's faith in Christ that pictures the washing away of our sins. Peter writes in a similar way saying that baptism saves us.

(1 Peter 3:21) The like figure whereunto even baptism doth also now save us (not the putting away of the filth of the flesh, but the answer of a good conscience toward God,) by the resurrection of Jesus Christ:

It is apparent by his qualifying statements that he is likewise referring to salvation through what baptism pictures. In this case, it is the resurrection of Jesus Christ that provides our salvation. When a believer is baptized, he is testifying, not of the body being cleaned of dirt, but of a conscience that has been cleansed from the defilement of sin.

Paul writes to Titus declaring that we have been saved by the Lord's regenerating work, which causes both a washing or a cleansing and a renewing of the Holy Spirit.

(Titus 3:5) Not by works of righteousness which we have done, but according to his mercy he saved us, by the washing of regeneration, and renewing of the Holy Ghost;

6) Promise of future resurrection

Baptism is the believer's testimony. He has a promise of tomorrow as well as the present certainty of the Lord's presence through His Spirit. 1 Corinthians 15 is considered the great resurrection chapter. It begins with the gospel, proceeds to describe the certainty of Christ's resurrection, encourages faithful living, and concludes with the believer being given a new body. Every believer will be changed (15:51).

(1 Corinthians 15:52) In a moment, in the twinkling of an eye, at the last trump: for the trumpet shall sound, and the dead shall be raised incorruptible, and we shall be changed.

Perhaps not as obvious is the promise of the believer's future resurrection from the grave. Just as Christ was raised from the grave and lifted up to heaven, we who are in Christ have the certainty of being raised, or possibly raptured, and caught up to be with Christ forever.

Every believer's baptism testifies that death is not the end. Because Christ was raised and His body glorified, so shall every believer be given a new body and unending life. According to Jesus Christ and His gospel, death is entrance into life with Him.

Based upon these promises, Paul gives a final exhortation. What we do for Christ counts. Life has meaning.

(1 Corinthians 15:58) Therefore, my beloved brethren, be ye stedfast, unmoveable, always abounding in the work of the Lord, forasmuch as ye know that your labour is not in vain in the Lord.

The Lord's Supper

(1 Corinthians 11:23) ...That the Lord Jesus the same night in which he was betrayed took bread:

The Lord's Supper was instituted on the night of the Lord's betrayal. This is the historical context. He could have said, "on the eve of the Passover" or "on the night before the crucifixion." But in mentioning the betrayal of Jesus, he reminds us of the ugliness of sin and the purpose of Christ's death.

The night Jesus instituted the Lord's Supper was not an ordinary night. Once a year the Jewish people celebrate Passover, which commemorates God's deliverance of the Israelites from Egypt. The Lord's Supper is the New Testament parallel to the Passover feast because it too celebrates God's delivering power, though in a greater way. Through the blood of Christ, we are delivered from the bondage of sin and are given freedom to serve the Son of God.

The Lord's Supper became the normal celebration of the early church (Acts 2:41-42). The early church was involved in four basic activities: teaching the revelation the apostles had received from God, fellowshipping, observing the Lord's Supper (breaking of bread), and praying.

The breaking of bread became synonymous with a fellowship meal. The early church incorporated the Supper established by Jesus at the end of their fellowship meals. The word "communion" is the same as "fellowship." Eventually that combination of a fellowship meal and communion became known as a Christian "love feast."

> *(1 Corinthians 10:16, 20-21) The cup of blessing which we bless, is it not the **communion** of the blood of Christ? The bread which we break, is it not the **communion** of the body of Christ? ...But I say, that the things which the Gentiles sacrifice, they sacrifice to devils, and not to God: and I would not that ye should have **fellowship** with devils. ²¹Ye cannot drink the cup of the Lord, and the cup of devils: ye cannot be partakers of the Lord's table, and of the table of devils.*

1) Memorializes Christ's death

> *(1 Corinthians 11:24-25) ...when he had given thanks, he brake it, and said, Take, eat: this is my body, which is broken for you: this do in remembrance of me. ²⁵After the same manner also he took the cup, when he had supped, saying, This cup is the new testament in my blood: this do ye, as oft as ye drink it, in remembrance of me.*

In speaking of His body and His blood, we have a reminder of His life and His death. At His incarnation, our Lord became the man Christ Jesus (1 Tim. 2:5) who lived a sinless life. He willingly laid down His life, shedding His blood for the sins of all mankind (1 Tim. 2:6).

And so, the references to His body and blood speak to His person and work. He was the God-man who became the mediator between God and mankind. As man He was qualified as our representative. Because He is God, His death perfectly and infinitely provided salvation for all who believe in Him.

To "remember" Him is to deliberately recall who He is and what He has done for us. We remember the miracles used to authenticate His Person, as well as His teachings, commands, and promises. Because we believers have the mind of Christ, we are now capable of grasping the truths of God which were concealed from us prior to conversion due to our sinful blindness (1 Cor. 2:16).

To remember Christ is to look beyond the historical event on Calvary. Yes, we are to look to the cross, but also to the implications of the cross we read in the Scriptures. We must remember what He has done for us personally, and how that constrains us to live for Him daily.

2) Pictures the life of faith in and dependence on Christ

> *(John 6:33) For the bread of God is he which cometh down from heaven, and giveth life unto the world.*

> *(John 6:47-48) Verily, verily, I say unto you, He that believeth on me hath everlasting life. I am that bread of life.*

> *(John 6:57) As the living Father hath sent me, and I live by the Father: so he that eateth me, even he shall live by me.*

Just as the picture of baptism raises us to follow Christ, so the symbols of the bread and the cup enable us to continue in fellowship with Him. The bread symbolizes our continued trust and dependence, while the cup reminds us of our need for confession and cleansing.

3) Pictures the fellowship of the saints with Christ and with others

Not only does the Lord's Supper emphasize the personal relationship of every believer with Christ, it recognizes the relationship of believers to one another. Remembering Christ affects our relation to others in the local church.

The Lord's Supper celebrates the communion of all saints (1 Cor. 10:15-21). The word "communion" (15) is the same word later, and in many places, translated "fellowship" (20). Believers are said to be "one bread" and "one body" (17) because we all partake of life from the same "one bread" (17) person, Jesus Christ.

As "partakers of the Lord's Table" (10:21), believers are to discern or recognize the Lord's body (1 Cor. 11:29). Those who eat and drink without discerning the body of the Lord, His church, eat and drink judgment on themselves.

The Corinthians are previously warned that those who destroy the temple of God, the church, God will destroy (1 Cor 3:16-17). This is a severe warning about bringing harm to the work of God through the church. The immediate context calls for the Corinthians to make a positive contribution by putting others first. They are to come together to remember what the Lord has done for them and to celebrate life in the body, that is, the church. Social standing is set aside, and all have equal standing in Christ. There is no preferential treatment of any members; all are recipients of Christ's blessings.

Discernment of the Lord's body is one of the most remarkably encouraging truths in the Bible. Jesus served His disciple's bread and the fruit of the vine as symbols of 1) His person and work and of 2) the divine union which took place between Himself and His believing followers. It is through this ordinance that believers are reminded that we not only belong to Him, but we also belong to one another.

4) Symbolizes Christ's broken body and shed blood

> (1 Corinthians 11:24) And when he had given thanks, he brake it, and said, Take, eat: this is my body, which is broken for you: this do in remembrance of me.

Clearly, the Lord was speaking metaphorically. As He spoke, He was standing before them holding bread and grape juice. His blood was still circulating in His body. Undoubtedly, the un-leavened bread and essentially unfermented grape juice are symbolic elements.

- Unleavened bread

32

The Passover required unleavened bread. Leaven pictures sin, and there is no doubt that the Lord intended the illustration to represent His sinless character and life.

> *(1 Corinthians 5:6-8) Your glorying is not good. Know ye not that a little leaven leaveneth the whole lump? ⁷Purge out therefore the old leaven, that ye may be a new lump, as ye are unleavened. For even Christ our passover is sacrificed for us: ⁸Therefore let us keep the feast, not with old leaven, neither with the leaven of malice and wickedness; but with the unleavened bread of sincerity and truth.*

- Unfermented fruit of the vine

There has been much debate on the character of the "cup." The common word for wine (*oinos*) is never used in reference to the Lord's Supper. Those who argue for the use of fermented juice or wine, haven't given a satisfactory explanation as to why that would be.

Under Old Testament law, Passover observance was required. Jewish practice involved the consumption of large quantities of juice which would suggest the use of essentially non-alcoholic juice. Perhaps a more thorough answer would involve the study of Jewish practices for preserving grape juice as a paste and the diluting of wine. However, it seems clear that the divine intention is to have a cup that is essentially non-alcoholic.

Many consider the use of unfermented juice for the Lord's Supper to be important so as not to be a source of temptation, nor an offense to any. No one should want to expose God's people to the first taste of alcohol at church! The church is made up of those from very sinful backgrounds. The reference of "such were some of you" (1 Cor. 6:11) included drunkards who may be tempted to their old life.

Furthermore, for Jesus, our High Priest, to have served alcoholic wine at the last Supper would have violated the Law in forbidding high priests to drink when officiating before the Lord. (Heb. 4:14-16; 5:1-10; Lev. 10:8-10).

5) Prophesies of His return implying our future deliverance

There is an explicit statement that the Lord's Supper is to be perpetuated until the Lord returns. And so, we celebrate in anticipation that He is returning!

> *(1 Corinthians 11:26) For as often as ye eat this bread, and drink this cup, ye do shew the Lord's death till he come.*

Jesus will return for believers, and they will eat with Him in Heaven (Matt. 26:29; Mk. 14:25; Lk. 22:16; 1 Cor. 11:26).

Each of the ordinances was commanded by Christ to be observed in the churches. The Bible evidence is that there is no such thing as a sacrament and that all obedient disciples of Christ should observe these ordinances. Each Christian should make sure that he has been scripturally baptized after his salvation. Among other teachings, Scripture uses the Lord's Supper to teach us that we should hate sin and walk closely with the Lord (1 Cor. 5:7-11; 10:14-22; 11:27-32).

3

The Ordinances Teach Us about Christ

As we have seen, the Lord's Supper and baptism are "ordinances" rather than "sacraments." At the core of sacramentalism is the belief that the "sacraments" are a means of grace or that they convey spiritual benefits to the participants. Baptists see no soteriological benefits in the ordinances; they are not a means of either justification or sanctification.

Baptists react strongly against any attempt to associate spiritual transactions with physical or ecclesiastical activities. There is no soteriological benefit to being baptized or in partaking of the Lord's Supper. The ordinances picture the benefits of God's gift of salvation in Jesus Christ, but they do not confer, add to, or perfect one's salvation.

The ordinances speak of His person and work.

Baptism

Only immersion adequately pictures the person and work of Jesus Christ. While many argue for another mode of baptism based upon the Old Testament rite of circumcision, it is clear that these two are distinct and unrelated.

Baptism is clearly not a replacement for circumcision. Baptism includes both males and females, while circumcision is exclusive to biological males. Baptism is for those who have personally believed, whereas circumcision is for eight-day-old infants as well as adult male proselytes. Circumcision was primarily a Jewish rite under the Old Testament Mosaic Law, but baptism is for believers in all nations. Baptism being associated with the Great Commission shows Jesus' compassion for all mankind. He came to be the Savior of the whole world.

In baptism we have something new and distinct from God's dealings with Israel. The command to disciple all nations, followed by baptizing and teaching these disciples, calls for the establishment of churches worldwide. The true followers of God now associate together in local churches. This is quite different than the centralized worship in Jerusalem's Temple.

By insisting that baptism is immersion and only immersion, Baptists are implicitly arguing that baptism is symbolic, not sacramental. Baptists believe that the main significance about baptism is its ability to picture Christ's death, burial, and resurrection, and the believer's identification with Christ in all aspects. This is the essence of the gospel.

> *(1 Corinthians 15:1-4) Moreover, brethren, I declare unto you the gospel which I preached unto you, which also ye have received, and wherein ye stand; [2]By which also ye are saved, if ye keep in memory what I preached unto you, unless ye have believed in vain. [3]For I delivered unto you first of all that which I also received, how that Christ died for our sins according to the Scriptures; [4]And that he was buried, and that he rose again the third day according to the Scriptures:*

The essence of the gospel is that Christ died for our sins. He was alive and He really died. His death was not for His sins because He had no sin. His was a redemptive death. He died that believers might be forgiven.

The fact that He was buried proves that He was dead. His case appeared hopeless. Even His disciples scattered in fear and despair. But His case was not hopeless; He was raised from the dead! He conquered death, proving His deity and that He will make good on His promise to give all believers life.

Through baptism we identify with Christ. Our case was hopeless with no way of escaping death and its consequences. But through Christ we are raised from spiritual death to enjoy life in Him. We may die physically, but death has lost its sting; it has no power over those who have trusted Jesus Christ. Death now becomes an entrance into the glorious presence of God.

This, and much more, is what baptism pictures for the believer.

Lord's Supper

Christ clearly teaches that the bread of the Lord's Supper represents His body and the cup represents His blood shed for us. The Lord's Supper is not getting in touch with your inner being. It is not mysticism. It is rooted in historical facts. Jesus lived. He had a body and a heart that pumped blood.

The unleavened bread pictures His sinless humanity guaranteed through the virgin birth. His body was prepared by God for sacrifice because the blood of bulls and goats was never sufficient without the blood of Jesus (Heb. 10:5-7).

The cup represents the blood of God's perfect Lamb. Yes, He was really human, and He really died. But His death was for all of mankind, but especially for those who believe. As His redeemed children, we celebrate what He has done for us.

In partaking of these elements, we proclaim the Lord's death until He comes. He died and was buried but He was raised again. He is alive! He is coming again!

The ordinances speak of our faith in His person and work.

Baptism

As already stated, baptism is for those who have consciously trusted in Christ. Baptism is a believer's own testimony of God's cleansing and regenerating work. It is also a visual message to all who witness the act and an assurance to the church of the credibility of the convert's profession. It not only witnesses to all observers, it becomes a permanent reminder to the one being baptized of his new life and new commitment to Christ. Consider the following from Warns:

> It (baptism) becomes to him (the believer) a God-willed, concise expression of his inner experience as a believer and of his new, God-given standing. ...a permanent reminder of his passage out of death into life, of his renunciation of the world and sin and of his surrender unto the Lord.[19]

> It is not my work, but in baptism I declare that I am come to an end of my own works and have ceased therefrom as one dead; and that my life, my strength, yea, every blessing I ascribe to Christ, and owe to Him Who died for me, yea, rather, has risen again for me.[20]

> But whoever submitted to baptism not only thereby acknowledged his faith in the Lord, but that he desired to belong to Him, that henceforth he would no more live, unto himself, but unto Him who for his sake had died and risen again (Rom 6:4; 8:13).[21]

> The man sees himself torn out of his former world; his life takes another direction, with another goal. The old has passed away; all things are become new. ...there is now given through baptism the testimony that: with Christ I am dead, buried, risen.[22]

---

[19] Warns, *Baptism*, 26.
[20] Ibid, 27.
[21] Ibid, 28.
[22] Ibid, 29.

Lord's Supper

> *(1 Corinthians 11:24-25) And when he had given thanks, he brake it, and said, Take, eat: this is my body, which is broken for you:* **this do in remembrance of me.** *[25]After the same manner also he took the cup, when he had supped, saying, This cup is the new testament in my blood:* **this do** *ye, as oft as ye drink it,* **in remembrance of me.**

The Lord's Supper is for believers. This is clear through both the setting of its observance and its participants. The Supper was instituted among the Lord's disciples who were called to remember His person and work. Christ's most important work at Calvary was still future to them but once accomplished would become the focus of their remembrance. Spurgeon powerfully states,

> It is not a converting ordinance, nor a saving ordinance; it is an establishing ordinance and a comforting ordinance for those who are saved. But it never was intended to save souls, neither is it adapted to that end; and if it be so misrepresented, it is apt rather to be the means of damning than of saving the soul, for he that so eats and drinks may, in very deed, be eating and drinking damnation to himself.[23]

Today, believers remember Him for His redemptive work on their behalf. One cannot remember something that has not been experienced. Therefore, the Lord's Supper is for those who have been transformed by God's grace through faith in the substitutionary atonement of Jesus Christ on the cross.

1) The Lord's Supper is a time for meditation

The Lord said twice, "This do … in remembrance of me" (1 Cor. 11:24-25). It is a time not only to thank but also to think, that is to mediate on and to contemplate what Jesus has done for us.

To the Israelite, the concept of remembering was more than

---

[23] Charles Spurgeon, "Fencing the Table," 1876, https://biblebb.com/files /spurgeon/2865.htm.

simply recalling something experienced in the past. It meant taking appropriate action in response to the person, event, or teaching. Jesus was commanding that Christians ponder the meaning of His life and death on their behalf. Practically, to remember Him is to think about His work in your personal life, considering the fruit of the gospel in both your justification and sanctification.

Paul exhorted Timothy to put the brethren in remembrance by being nourished up in the words of faith. In the book of Deuteronomy, the key word is "remember." It is used at least sixteen times, and the word "forget" is used nine times as God warns Israel of His commands.

Of the many exhortations to remember, the Psalmist's words to Israel provide a focus. To remember is to meditate, to think or ponder the truths of God's commands and His works.

> *(Psalm 77:11-12) I will remember the works of the LORD: surely I will remember thy wonders of old. ¹²I will meditate also of all thy work, and talk of thy doings.*

The opposite of remembering God and His works would be to forget Him.

> *(Psalm 78:11) And forgat his works, and his wonders that he had shewed them.*

The command to remember calls us to submission and obedience; it calls for our best and complete response to God. But in contrast to remembering, forgetting implies that we have departed from God's way; we are now subjects of His chastening rather than recipients of His blessed fellowship and tender care.

In Scripture, to remember is more than a mere mental action of reflection. When God remembered Noah (Gen. 8:1), it was a statement of His ongoing care during Noah's days on the ark. Similarly, in the New Testament, Paul's ministry to the Gentiles involved remembering the poor (Gal. 2:14). This was more than having sympathetic feelings for those suffering; it was a call to action in relieving their suffering. And so, remembering Jesus involves more than a reminder of who He was and what He did on the cross. It is a call to self-examination of our personal walk and rededication to the purposes of God.

Remembering Jesus Christ includes at least two concepts. It first calls for recognizing and reinforcing the teachings pertaining to His person and work. Second, it requires examining my life in relation to His perfect character and committing myself to advancing the purpose of His work. On one hand, this involves confession of sin and restoration of fellowship, and on the other, service to Him both in and through the local church in the work of evangelism and edification.

2) The two symbols remind us what our salvation cost.

The Bread

> *(John 6:47-48) Verily, verily, I say unto you, He that believeth on me hath everlasting life. 48I am that bread of life.*

In this memorial meal, the bread is eaten first. The bread is symbolic of Christ's body. It reminds us that God became flesh—a man—that He might be our Savior. He suffered for us bodily, and as the Bread of God, He is sufficient to meet our every need.

When Jesus said, "this is my body, which is broken for you" He was declaring that He, as the incarnate Son of God, was giving His life for us. The words "for you" are both instructive and powerful. Christ did not suffer and die for Himself but for lost mankind. Charles Wesley wrote, "Amazing love! How can it be that Thou, my God shouldst die for me?"

The bread also speaks to us of Christ's presence with us. What we eat becomes a part of us. When we believed, He indwelt us by His Spirit and is always with us. Jesus said His food was to do the will of God. We are to remember His presence with us as we do His will and live a life of dependence on Him.

> *(John 6:57) As the living Father hath sent me, as I live by the Father: so he that eateth me, even he shall live by me.*

Many verses in John 6 teach that we are to live a life of continued faith in Christ (6:29,33,53,57). He is sufficient for all trials and all needs.

As we have seen, the bread speaks to us of our mutual faith; we are one bread.

> *(1 Corinthians 10:17) For we being many are **one bread**, and one body: for we are all partakers of that one bread.*

> *(Matthew 26:27) And he took the cup, and gave thanks, and gave it to them, saying, Drink **ye all** of it; [or "Drink of it, all of you"]*

This was a big problem in Corinth. They were eating without regard to their brethren. They were not demonstrating the love of Christ in their Christian relationships.

The Cup

The cup is filled with the fruit of the vine, which symbolizes the blood of Christ. Christ's life blood was shed on the cross as a payment for our sin. Without the shedding of blood there is no remission or forgiveness of sin. Christ's blood, poured out, speaks of the forgiveness for sins. Because of His shed blood, we can now be fully and freely forgiven by God.

> *(Ephesians 1:7) In whom we have redemption through his blood, the forgiveness of sins, according to the riches of his grace;*

> *(1 Peter 1:18-19) Forasmuch as ye know that ye were not redeemed with corruptible things, as silver and gold, from your vain conversation received by tradition from your fathers; [19]But with the precious blood of Christ, as of a lamb without blemish and without spot:*

While communion is a reminder of Christ's work in the past, the emphasis of the Lord's Supper seems to be the present application of Christ's death. Though forgiven and assured of eternal life, the believer needs daily cleansing from sin in order to walk in fellowship with God.

John's account of Christ washing the disciples' feet makes the distinction between the washing of regeneration and the cleansing of daily sin. The cup of the Lord's Supper illustrates the need for regular cleansing. We still need to apply the cup daily. Repentance and confession of sin is a regular exercise of the Christian.

> *(1 John 1:9) If we confess our sins, he is faithful and just to forgive us our sins, and to cleanse us from all unrighteousness.*

The cup symbolizes the propitiation effected by the death of Christ. God is satisfied by the suffering of Jesus Christ in the place of every believer. He is the fulfillment of the Passover Lamb for all who will trust in His bloody death for them. Now the believer is accepted in the Beloved One, Jesus Christ, and has boldness to enter the holy presence of God (Heb. 10:19). Jesus, as mediator between God and man (1 Tim. 2:5), provides access to God by His Spirit through faith and prayer (Rom. 5:2; Eph. 2:18; 3:12).

3) The Lord's Supper is a time for proclamation

> *(1 Corinthians 11:26) For as often as ye eat this bread, and drink this cup, ye **do shew** the Lord's death till he come.*

Paul does not tell how often we ought to observe the Lord's Supper, but he does tell us that we should regularly observe the Lord's Supper on a continuing, permanent basis.

The Lord's Table is rich in meaning. We show or proclaim the death of Christ every time we remember Him in communion. The church is reminded, our children are taught, and unsaved observers hear that God became man and died a substitutionary death, satisfying God's righteous judgment for sins, so that whoever believes in Him will have everlasting life (John 3:16).

The Lord's Table is not only a look back, but also a look ahead. The same Lord who died to save us is coming again to receive us to Himself. We celebrate this ordinance until He comes; then we will commune with Him in His presence forever.

4) The Lord's Supper is a time for examination

> *(1 Corinthians 11:28) But let a man examine himself, and so let him eat of that bread, and drink of that cup.*

The purpose of the Lord's Supper is so that we keep in our active memory what Jesus has done for us. But its practice accomplishes more than that. Believers are regularly held to account for their personal walk and faithfulness. Because it is a church ordinance, it requires the regular evaluation of church relationships and responsibilities as well. These things make it a priority for the church and must be observed on a regular basis.

The Lord's Table is a comprehensive ordinance. In it we remember Christ's person and work, we confess sin and renew our commitment to Him, we proclaim the gospel, and we look forward to His return.

Consideration of the most problematic Lord's Supper passage

> *(John 6:53-54) Then Jesus said unto them, Verily, verily, I say unto you, Except ye eat the flesh of the Son of man, and drink his blood, ye have no life in you. ⁵⁴Whoso eateth my flesh, and drinketh my blood, hath eternal life; and I will raise him up at the last day.*

John 6:53-54 is the basic text that supposedly supports the Roman Catholic Mass. Catholicism teaches that the wine and bread are literally changed into the blood and body of Jesus Christ—that Christ is literally there and consumed by the person who involves himself in the Mass and the Eucharist. In this heretical teaching, each Mass is a new sacrifice of Jesus Christ for our sins.

The priest says in Latin, "Hoc es corpus meum," meaning, "This is my body." The words "hocus pocus" come from the mocking of transubstantiation by the general populace and picked up by magicians. It is all trickery!

Unwilling to repudiate the receiving of grace through the elements, Reformed churches teach a variation of this. Presbyterians do not believe that the elements of bread and wine are physically changed into Christ's body and blood, as Catholicism teaches, but they hold that the elements are more than mere symbols or reminders of Jesus. They teach that as we partake of the bread and wine, we encounter Jesus, who is spiritually, authentically present in the sacrament.[24]

However, Jesus is not talking of drinking His blood literally as is the Catholic teaching, or mystically as viewed by Reformed Churches. Literal drinking would be against the prohibition on consuming blood, as any good Jew would know. Jesus is giving an illustration; eating and drinking are analogies. In the common vernacular, when someone hears information they do not believe or a truth they are unwilling to accept, they say, "I can't swallow that" or "That's something I just can't swallow." Here the Lord is saying that if you're not willing to "swallow" or believe His shed blood for sin, you can't come to Him.

Words are not to be understood literally

These words (*eat flesh, drink blood*) are not to be understood literally. Often in the Gospel of John, Jesus spoke to men in spiritual terms, and men understood Him in merely literal terms. For example, Jesus spoke to the Jerusalem Jewish leaders about "destroying this temple" in chapter 2, and they took Him to be referring to the literal temple, while He was referring to the "temple" of His body (2:19-22). In chapter 3, Jesus spoke to Nicodemus about being "born again," and once again He was taken literally. Nicodemus wanted to know how he could enter the second time into the womb. Jesus spoke to the woman at the well about "living water," and she thought it was literally something to drink (John 4:10-15). She asked how he was going to draw from the deep well without a bucket. In John 6, Jesus is speaking to the Jews about "eating" His "flesh," which is the "bread of life," and many of them take His words in a very literal way. They're thinking of cannibalism.

---

[24] Paul Galbreath, "Sacraments: Grace We Can Touch" (*Presbyterians Today*, June 2014), 34.

Words are to be understood metaphorically

Spurgeon said, "It is a very beautiful and simple metaphor."[25]

> *(John 6:51) I am the living bread which came down from heaven: if any man eat of this bread, he shall live for ever: and the bread that I will give is my flesh, which I will give for the life of the world.*

Eating is the taking into yourself something which exists externally, which you receive and which becomes a part of yourself and which helps to build up and sustain you. That something supplies a great need; when you receive it, it nourishes your life. That is the essence of the metaphor and it well describes the act and the result of faith.

"Flesh" speaks of the uniqueness of His person; it refers to the reality of His Incarnation.

> *(1 John 4:2) Hereby know ye the Spirit of God: Every spirit that confesseth that Jesus Christ is come in the flesh is of God:*

> *(2 John 7) For many deceivers are entered into the world, who confess not that Jesus Christ is come in the flesh. This is a deceiver and an antichrist.*

Even today, we use the terms "flesh and blood," to indicate an actual person. In the passage, Christ repeatedly says "I am the bread of life." From verses 30 to 51 Jesus is saying one thing: your souls are hungry, God sent bread, and I am that bread.

> *(John 6:33) For the bread of God is he which cometh down from heaven, and giveth life unto the world.*

> *(John 6:35) And Jesus said unto them, I am the bread of life: he that cometh to me shall never hunger; and he that believeth on me shall never thirst.*

> *(John 6:47) Verily, verily, I say unto you, He that believeth on me hath everlasting life.*

---

[25] Charles Spurgeon, "Truly Eating the Flesh of Jesus." Sermon No. 1288. delivered April 9, 1876. https:// www.spurgeongems.org/sermon/chs2638.pdf.

(John 6:48) I am that bread of life.

(John 6:51) I am the living bread which came down from heaven: if any man eat of this bread, he shall live for ever: and the bread that I will give is my flesh, which I will give for the life of the world.

We see two truths here. 1) Jesus proclaims His true nature. The nature of Christ is seen in His description as the living bread. We also see 2) the source of Christ is stated as *from heaven.* Jesus Christ says, "I came to this earth as living bread for souls that are hungry. I am that bread to nourish your hungry, growling, unsatisfied soul."

1) Giving of flesh and blood

Giving of His flesh, along with reference to the blood, points to the substitutionary atonement. We must believe in the death of the Incarnate Son of God.

(John 6:51) I give for the life of the world.

Therefore, He's talking prophetically about His cross. He's saying, "I'm going to give my flesh." He's soon to become a vicarious sacrifice for sin. He's going to offer His own flesh on the cross; He's talking about His crucifixion.

(1 Peter 2:24) Who his own self bare our sins in his own body on the tree, that we, being dead to sins, should live unto righteousness: by whose stripes ye were healed.

(2 Corinthians 5:21) For he hath made him to be sin for us, who knew no sin; that we might be made the righteousness of God in him.

(1 John 2:2) And he is the propitiation for our sins: and not for ours only, but also for the sins of the whole world.

(1 Timothy 2:6) Who gave himself a ransom for all, to be testified in due time.

Jesus says, "I will give" two times in verse 51. He says that He will give His flesh for the life of the world." His was a voluntary sacrifice.

(John 10:18) No man taketh it from me, but I lay it down of myself. I have power to lay it down, and I have power to take it again. This commandment have I received of my Father.

And so, flesh speaks of the uniqueness of His person (1 John 4:2), while the giving of His flesh, along with reference to the blood, points to the substitutionary atoning work.

2) Eating and drinking are calls to faith and dependence

For any person to come to Jesus Christ he must be willing to accept the purpose and value of Christ's shed blood on the cross. That's what He's saying to these Jews. He's saying you not only have to accept His person, but you've also got to be willing to swallow His substitutionary sacrifice.

This is repugnant to many people because it speaks of the sinfulness of the human race and the sinfulness of the human heart. The bloody sacrificial death of Jesus was necessary because of the repugnant, hideous, repulsive, vile human depravity which is the nature of us all. Eating the flesh and drinking the blood of Christ means, we must believe in the death of the Incarnate Son of God for our forgiveness and eternal life.

From the words of Jesus in John 6, we understand that coming is the same as believing (35); believing gives life, that is, eternal life (40, 47); and eating the bread or his flesh gives eternal life; one lives forever (51, 54).

Euclid was the father of Geometry. According to Euclid's first notion, things equal to the same thing are equal to each other (A = B and B = C, then A = C). This notion or axiom supports the conclusion that *eating* in this passage is a metaphor for faith. Therefore, eating His flesh equals believing in Him. By comparison of verses 40 and 54, both believing and eating produce the same result; I will "raise him up at the last day."

John 6 closes with the words of Peter saying "thou hast the words of eternal life" and "we believe." The disciples believed Jesus to be Messiah and God! Peter's words indicate that he got it; he understood. He speaks of words and believing (68-69), and not of literal eating. Peter understands that Jesus' words are the basis of life (63). ***Therefore, we confirm that eating His flesh is the same as believing in Him.***

Like Peter, Baptists also understand! Our celebration of the Lord's Supper involves symbolism. When we take the cup, we are declaring our ongoing need for cleansing and forgiveness as we seek to live in daily fellowship with God (1 John 1:9). In eating the bread which represents His body, we are reminded of our need to daily depend upon Him. Ours is to be a life of faith in Christ. He alone has the power to transform lives as pictured in baptism. He alone is the bread that can fill the hunger of the heart as pictured in the Lord's Supper.

> *(John 6:34-35) Then said they unto him, Lord, evermore give us this bread. ³⁵And Jesus said unto them, I am the bread of life: he that cometh to me shall never hunger; and he that believeth on me shall never thirst.*

Jesus says that He is the bread that will give eternal satisfaction. Those coming to Him shall never hunger and those believing will never thirst. Note the parallelism. Here, coming is equal to believing.

Jesus said to those Jews who were fed the day before, "You don't need to worry about physical food." They had followed Him to Capernaum because their stomachs were growling, and it was morning and time for breakfast. But physical food would never satisfy their deepest need.

> *(John 6:27) Labour not for the meat which perisheth, but for that meat which endureth unto everlasting life, which the Son of man shall give unto you: for him hath God the Father sealed.*

Christ tells them, "Don't work for that kind of food; you need the food that satisfies the soul." Then He says, "God sent that food and I am that food."

The Lord's Supper was to show the Lord's death; it not only pictures or represents it, but it proclaims it as well. John uses similar symbolism in his first epistle when he speaks of Jesus the

Son coming by water and blood. This is a reference to His Person and work (1 John 5:6). In the waters of baptism, He was declared to be God's beloved Son who must be heard. In His bloody death on the cross, He must be believed!

John 6 closes with "thou hast the words of eternal life" and "we believe." The disciples believed Jesus to be Messiah and God! And so, we know God through His words, the Bible, and by communicating with Him in prayer.

Peter's words indicate that he got it; he understood Christ's metaphor. And so today, we must understand this vital teaching as well.

3) Eating and drinking are a call to fellowship with Christ

Eating and drinking describe living in dependence.

> *(John 6:57) As the living Father hath sent me, and I live by the Father: so he that eateth me, even he shall live by me.*

The Lord is describing an ongoing, never-ending, personal relationship with Christ. When you receive Jesus Christ, you become one with Him! The believer is *in Christ*. Oh, what a wonderful thought!

> *(Galatians 2:20) I am crucified with Christ: nevertheless I live; yet not I, but Christ liveth in me: and the life which I now live in the flesh I live by the faith of the Son of God, who loved me, and gave himself for me.*

> *(Philippians 1:21) For to me to live is Christ, and to die is gain.*

As we go through this world, we are living lives of Christ; we are one with Him. He dwells in me; I dwell in Him. As such, there are similarities between Christ's relationship with His Father and our relationship with Christ. Notice the word "as" in John 6:57:

> *(John 6:57) As the living Father hath sent me, and I live by the Father: so he that eateth me, even he shall live by me.*

Because believers lack the attributes of deity, and will never be gods, we recognize a similarity of relationship and not an exact parallel. To be sure, the comparison is with the bread-flesh-person and not with the blood-work of Christ.

*(John 1:1) In the beginning was the Word, and the Word was **with God**, and the Word was God.*

The Son is God and was with God or face to face in fellowship with His Father. The Lord Jesus described His fellowship with the Father in other writings of John.

The Son's fellowship with the Father is both knowable and personal.

*(John 5:20) For the Father loveth the Son, and **sheweth him all things** that himself doeth: and he will shew him greater works than these, that ye may marvel.*

The Son's fellowship is satisfying.

(John 5:20) For the Father loveth the Son….

The Son's fellowship is enduring, inseparable, and empowering fellowship.

*(John 8:29) And he that sent me is with me: the Father hath **not left me alone**; for I do always those things that please him.*

For us, our relationship is secure, but it's also growing, developing, and sharing. The Son also testifies that He does "those things that please him." He is submissive and subordinate to the Father. Jesus was equal in deity but distinct. His role was not the same as His Father's role. The Father was directive in His fellowship with the Son.

*(1 John 4:14) And we have seen and do testify that **the Father sent the Son** to be the Saviour of the world.*

This fellowship was communicative.

*(John 11:41-42) Then they took away the stone from the place where the dead was laid. And Jesus lifted up his eyes, and said, Father, I thank thee that **thou hast heard me.** 42And **I knew that thou hearest me always**: but because of the people which stand by I said it, that they may believe that thou hast sent me.*

Conclusion: How do we go about "eating"?

If the bread of the Lord's Supper symbolizes our faith and dependence on Christ, how do we increase in both? How do we go about living a life of fellowship with and dependence in Christ?

1. Our physical eating times come several times a day.

We should partake of the flesh and blood of Jesus regularly by studying the word of God, confessing sin, and continuing in prayerfulness.

2. We should have set times for eating.

None of us are likely to flourish physically if we pick up our food randomly and have no regular meals. It is best to have settled times when you can sit down to the table and take your food properly.

3. There is pleasure in eating.

No healthy person needs to be threatened to make him or her eat. God has made eating a pleasurable experience. The taste buds are conscious of pleasure while we are eating. And truly, in fellowship and communion with Jesus there is a sweetness that saturates one's whole soul.

If ever you lose your taste for Christ, you can be sure that you are sick of soul. There can be no surer sign of a sad state of heart than not to delight in the Lord Jesus Christ.

- Find a quiet place.
- Establish a regular time.
- Determine some definite goals.

Those who do the common things—partaking of the word, praying, confessing, and obeying—uncommonly well, will grow in enjoyment of God.

Read the Bible. Read at the pace of the tongue and the ear, not at the pace of the mind's ability to grasp information. You are not reading for information; you are reading to allow God to enrich your soul.

Memorize and meditate on the written word of God. Look for what is significant about life. Meditating is stopping to notice what is important about God, about life, and about ministry to others.

To borrow words about the value of reading poetry,

> "Reading verse (or the Bible) rescues us from the mundaneness of life; it permits us to observe again with wonder, and shocks us out of our cynicism and joylessness. After a day in which we have been constantly distracted by electronic devices grasping our attention, or numbed by a 'to-do' list that makes our PDA sigh with despair, we read Robert Frost's..."[26]

We read the precious word of God and we are alive again with freshness—alive as His children, as members of His body. We are refreshed in hope, alert to His presence, appreciative of the beauty around us, and confident in His purposes. Without the Word, I am left to the loneliness of existence, the randomness of circumstances, and the meaninglessness of activity. Without God's word as the nourishment of my soul, I will, at best, live without spiritual power and purpose.

> "Mundaneness is, I believe, part of the curse of Genesis 3. The earth no longer yields its bounty without toilsome labor and much frustration. Our routines make us more efficient, as we attempt to scratch out some form of survival in this cursed environment, but those same routines can make us more like cogs in a machine and less like humans. Life becomes a series of tasks, with few uninterrupted moments to pause, to reflect, to appreciate."[27]

It is God's word "that enables us, through the fog of images and sounds, to again see ourselves and others as the bearers of the image of God.... It is precisely this longer look that is necessary to

---

[26] T. David Gordon. *Why Johnny Can't Preach: The Media Have Shaped the Messengers* (Phillipsburg, NJ: P&R Publishing, 2009), 52.
[27] Gordon, *Why Johnny Can't Preach*, 53.

cultivate a sensibility for the significant."[28]

Pray. As you talk with the Lord include adoration, thanksgiving, intercession, and personal requests for advance of the gospel and the church. The flesh opposes our prayer life because prayer is contrary to the old nature. Like trying to hold someone under water, the flesh surfaces to oppose our spiritual efforts to die to self and live in submission to the Savior. In prayer, we continually combat our human weakness, the hostile disaffection of our flesh, and external distractions.

Finding a place and time to be alone with God is not an easy assignment for anyone.

> *(Matthew 6:6) But thou, when thou prayest, enter into thy closet, and when thou hast shut thy door, pray to thy Father which is in secret; and thy Father which seeth in secret shall reward thee openly.*

> *(Psalm 63:1) O God, thou art my God; early will I seek thee: my soul thirsteth for thee, my flesh longeth for thee in a dry and thirsty land, where no water is;*

You can either pray or sleep. You can have spiritual power and victory, or you can continue in defeat. The world will grip you. The flesh will master you. The devil will deceive you.

> *(Luke 22:40) And when he was at the place, he said unto them, Pray that ye enter not into temptation.*

> *(Luke 22:46) And said unto them, Why sleep ye? rise and pray, lest ye enter into temptation.*

If you want to remain defeated or experience a great fall, sleep on! But if you want spiritual growth, power, and fruitfulness— pray!

> *(Psalm 5:3) My voice shalt thou hear in the morning, O LORD; in the morning will I direct my prayer unto thee, and will look up.*

---

[28] Gordon, *Why Johnny Can't Preach*, 53.

Just as the Father sent the Son from heaven and the Son lives out the life of the Father, so the one who "eats" and "drinks" the Son, lives because of the Son. The Father's life extends to and through the Son to those who will partake of the Son's flesh and blood— and who do so daily. He alone has the power to transform lives. He alone is the bread that can fill the hunger of the heart. He can change your life. He alone can satisfy your soul. The Lord's Supper pictures this relationship and reminds believers of their spiritual blessings and responsibilities.

4

The Ordinances Teach Us
about The Church (Part 1)

Baptism of believers by immersion signifies entrance into the church.

In recent generations, baptism has often been termed "a secondary and non-essential doctrine" of Scripture. It is true that baptism is not essential to salvation, and it is also true that many who are genuinely born again are misled and confused about baptism. Yet, biblical baptism is essential in that it is commanded by the Lord Jesus Christ to be observed by all believers (Mat. 28:18-20). Immersion of believers is the only true baptism and the undisputed practice of the early church.

On Pentecost, Peter preached the gospel to the Jews gathered in Jerusalem resulting in three thousand souls being saved (Acts 2:41). Where did the apostles get the idea that converts should be baptized and added to the church? The answer is not a difficult one. They clearly understood the implications of the Great Commission which associated baptism with both conversion and church identification (Mat. 28:18-20). Baptism is a church ordinance.

Baptism of believers by immersion signifies entrance into the fellowship of the church.

It is the normal pattern in the book of Acts that believers were baptized and added to the membership of a local church (Acts 2:41). The early church practiced regenerate, immersed church membership (see Chapter 8). Baptism connects believers to the local church and gives them a real sense of being connected with others in both testimony and ministry.

Baptism is immersion in water.

Phillip Schaff, a Presbyterian, writes:

> **The usual form of baptism was immersion.** This is inferred from **the original meaning of the Greek...**; from the analogy of John's baptism in the Jordan; from the apostles' comparison of the sacred rite with the miraculous passage of the Red Sea, with the escape of the ark from the flood, with a cleansing and refreshing bath, and with **burial and resurrection**; finally, from **the general custom of the ancient church**, which prevails in the East to this day (emphasis added).[29]

The following is a typical doctrinal statement of Bible-believing Baptists concerning the ordinances.

> We believe that both Christian baptism and the Lord's Supper are each a symbolic memorial and a prophecy. We believe that **Christian baptism is the single immersion in water of a believer performed in the name of the Father, the Son, and the Holy Spirit.** It shows forth, in solemn and beautiful figure our faith in the crucified, buried, and risen Savior, and our death to sin and resurrection to a new life. **Baptism is prerequisite to the privileges of church membership and**

---

[29] Philip & David Schley Schaff, *History of the Christian Church Volume 1* (New York: Charles Scribner's Sons, 1910), 468-469.

| *participation in the Lord's Supper* (emphasis added).[30]

What was the historical practice?

It is not difficult to find pedobaptists (those who baptize infants) who acknowledge that immersion was the mode of baptism practiced by the apostles and the early churches. Although he argues that sprinkling is acceptable, Calvin states: ". . . it is evident that the term *baptise* means to immerse, and that this was the form used by the primitive Church."[31]

Methodist I. H. Marshall, writing to defend infant baptism, affirmed that immersion was practiced in the early church, stating:

> The most that can (and must) be said is that both modes of baptism, immersion (certainly) and affusion (at least from the third century) were practiced, depending on local circumstances.[32]

This statement agrees with historians from all denominational persuasions, and certainly all Baptists.

What is the meaning of the word?

In Martin Luther's *Order of Baptism*, we read: "Then he shall take the child and dip him in the font. . . ."[33] Likewise, in his journal, John Wesley affirmed the early church baptized by immersion, writing: "Mary Welsh, aged eleven days, was baptized, according to the custom of the first church and the rule of the Church of

---

[30] Leonard Woolsey Bacon, *A History of American Christianity* (New York, The Christian Literature Co., 1897), 221-222.

[31] John Calvin, *Institutes of the Christian Religion,* ch XV, no 19, trans. Norton, Allen, and Beveridge (Bellingham, WA: Logos Bible Software, 1997).

[32] Ian Howard Marshall, "The meaning of the verb 'to baptize'" (Evangelical Quarterly: An International Review of Bible and Theology, 45, 3, 1973), 130-140.

[33] Martin Luther, *Luther's Works, Volume 53: Liturgy and Hymns,* (Philadelphia: Fortress Press, 1965), 100.

England, by *immersion*."[34]

Moses Stuart, a Congregationalist, who taught at Andover Seminary, wrote a significant work on the mode of Baptism. He stated: "*Bapto* and *baptize* mean to dip, plunge, or immerse, into anything liquid. All lexicographers and critics of any note are agreed in this."[35]

Before the *King James Version* of the Bible became available in 1611, the Anabaptists and Protestants used the Geneva Bible of 1560. When King James enlisted fifty-four scholars to produce a new translation, he gave them fourteen rules that must govern their work. One of those rules required the old ecclesiastical words to be kept. The word *church* was not to be translated *assembly* or *congregation*, and *baptism* was to be maintained as a transliteration rather than translated *immersion*.[36]

The translators then came to the Greek word for *baptism* and opted to continue to use the word as it appeared in the Genevan Bible. Translating the Greek word would not only have violated King James' ruling, but would also have caused great difficulty in the state Anglican church. These men believed the Bible and had they translated literally, they would be acknowledging baptism to be immersion, which would have greatly upset the state church. Therefore, they continued to anglicize the Greek word by use of the word *baptism* even though every legitimate lexicon makes it clear that the Greek word literally means *to dip, to plunge, or to immerse*.

What does baptism picture?

The ordinance of baptism pictures the work of Christ and the salvation of the believing sinner as he identifies with Jesus Christ

---

[34] Nehemiah Curnock, ed., *The Journal of John Wesley, Vol. 1* (London: Epworth Press, 1938), 166.

[35] Moses Stuart, *Is the Mode of Christian Baptism Prescribed in the New Testament?* (Nashville: Graves, Mark & Rutland, 1856), 41.

[36] William Muir, *Our Grand Old Bible* (London: Morgan & Scott, Ltd. 1911), 97-8.

and His church.

Baptism is also a picture of the work of the Holy Spirit baptizing believers into the body of Christ, uniting them together for the work of Christ in the local church. And so, baptism pictures the believer's entrance into new life and into the church. The believer not only has a new life, but a new purpose, a new direction, and a new destination as well as a new family and fellowship. Warns observes,

> In the days of the apostles all men, Jews and heathen, sufficiently understood that baptism signified a death to the old sphere, life and god, with the entrance into a new sphere, a walking in newness of life, and full dedication to a new LORD. In general, the risks by persecution were such as to deter any but the sincere from being baptized, so that baptism could be safely administered at once upon confession of Christ as Lord...[37]

Baptism reminds the believer that he has experienced a permanent, once for all, and fundamental change! Often, as part of the baptismal experience, the candidate is asked, "Is it your desire and commitment to serve Him all the days of your life?"

What do the Scriptures say?

Immersion is clearly the proper mode of baptism. Not only does the word mean *to dip, submerge, or immerse,* but immersion is evident as the New Testament practice (Matt. 3:16; Mark 1:10; Acts 8:38,39). In fact, there is little argument of this among various church groups. There is also general agreement that, beyond the apostolic churches, the early church also practiced immersion.

Consider that John the Baptist baptized in a place of *much water* which would have been unnecessary if a small amount of water on the head would have been sufficient (John 3:23). In the case of Philip and the eunuch, they went down into the water, both the

---

[37] Warns, *Baptism*, 30.

administrator and the candidate (Acts 8:38). Only immersion would necessitate standing in the water to perform. The place of the baptism must have been at a site suitable for immersion. The body of water had to be large enough to accommodate both participants and deep enough so that the act of immersion could be performed.

Maybe the most obvious argument for baptism being immersion is that only this form pictures the death, burial, and resurrection of Jesus Christ. If you discard immersion, the picture is gone and later New Testament teaching on the Christian life is compromised as well. Consider Paul's epistles to the Romans and to the Colossians:

> (Romans 6:3-5) Know ye not, that so many of us as were baptized into Jesus Christ were baptized into his death? *4Therefore we are buried with him by baptism into death: that like as Christ was raised up from the dead by the glory of the Father, even so we also should walk in newness of life. 5For if we have been planted together in the likeness of his death, we shall be also in the likeness of his resurrection:*

> (Colossians 2:12) Buried with him in baptism, wherein also ye are risen with him through the faith of the operation of God, who hath raised him from the dead.

> (Colossians 3:1) If ye then be risen with Christ, seek those things which are above, where Christ sitteth on the right hand of God.

Martin Luther spoke of baptism as a symbol of death and resurrection, writing:

> For this reason *I would have those who are to be baptized completely immersed in the water*, as the word says and as the mystery indicates. Not because I deem this necessary, but because it would be well to give to a thing so perfect and complete a sign that is also complete and perfect. And *this is doubtless the way in which it was instituted by Christ. The sinner* does not so much need to be washed as he *needs to die*, in order to be wholly renewed and made another creature, *and*

> *to be conformed to the death and resurrection of Christ, with whom he dies and rises again through baptism* (emphasis added).[38]

The picture of baptism showing burial and resurrection demands that its form be immersion. But how many times is one put under and raised from the water? There are some who teach that the candidate should be immersed three times, once for each of three persons of the Trinity. At least one Christian group generally immerses forward rather than backward.

But what is the common way to bury someone who has died? Do we bury them multiple times? No, they are placed in the ground once and then covered with dirt. It would seem clear to most without argument that you only bury an individual once, not three times, and that you don't generally bury someone on their face.

The following is from the letter of explanation sent by Adoniram Judson to the Third (Congregational) Church in Plymouth, giving the major reasons for his newfound convictions concerning believer's immersion.

> I knew that I had been sprinkled in infancy and that this had been deemed baptism. But *throughout the whole New Testament I could find nothing that looked like sprinkling*, in connection with the ordinance of baptism. It appeared to me, that *if a plain person should without any previous information on the subject, read through the New Testament, he would never get the idea, that baptism consisted in sprinkling*. He would find that baptism, in all the cases particularly described, was administered in rivers, and the parties are represented as going down into the water, and coming up out of the water, which they would not have been so foolish as to do for the purpose of sprinkling.
>
> In regard to the word itself which is translated baptism, a very

---

[38] Martin Luther, *Three Treatises* (Philadelphia: Fortress Press, 1960), 191.

little search convinced me that its plain, appropriate meaning was immersion or dipping; and though I read extensively on the subject, *I could not find that any learned Pedobaptist had ever been able to produce an instance, from any Greek writer, in which it meant sprinkling, or anything but immersion,* accept in some figurative applications, which could not be fairly brought into the question (emphasis added).[39]

After studying what the Bible taught about baptism, Adoniram Judson became a Baptist and the first Baptist missionary sent from this young nation. He left as a Congregationalist but served as a Baptist, having committed himself to the New Testament pattern for his ministry in Burma.

Baptism is because of faith in Jesus Christ.

From its inception the early church required converts to make a verbal profession of faith in the Lord Jesus Christ. Following Philip's explanation of Isaiah 53, the Ethiopian was convinced that Jesus was the Messiah, and he was marvelously converted. Perhaps this court official became the first black convert to the Christian faith. It was only after his confession that he was immersed.

> *(Acts 8:36-39) And as they went on their way, they came unto a certain water: and the eunuch said, **See, here is water; what doth hinder me to be baptized?** [37]And Philip said, If thou believest with all thine heart, thou mayest. And he answered and said, **I believe that Jesus Christ is the Son of God.** [38]And he commanded the chariot to stand still: and they went down both into the water, both Philip and the eunuch; and he baptized him. [39]And when they were come up out of the water, the Spirit of the Lord caught away Philip, that the eunuch saw him no more: and he went on his way rejoicing.*

---

[39] Francis Wayland, *A Memoir of the Life and Labors of the Rev. Adoniram Judson, D.D., Vol. I* (Boston: Phillips, Sampson, and Company, 1853), 102-103. Cited by Dr. David Cummins, *This Day in Baptist History Volume One, 69.*

In making sure that the eunuch is a believer, Philip clarifies that baptism is not a saving rite. He says, "If thou believest with all thing heart, thou mayest." Whereupon the eunuch made a frank and bold confession of faith: "I believe that Jesus Christ is the Son of God."

The pattern of believing prior to immersion is seen years later at Corinth.

> *(Acts 18:7-8) And he departed thence, and entered into a certain man's house, named Justus, one that worshipped God, whose house joined hard to the synagogue. ⁸And Crispus, the chief ruler of the synagogue, **believed on the Lord** with all his house; and many of the Corinthians **hearing believed, and were baptized**.*

Faith is a heart matter that is expressed by verbal confession. Baptism is the testimony of one's expressed faith, the ordinance itself being an open confession of belief in the Lord Jesus Christ.

> *(Romans 10:10) For with the heart man believeth unto righteousness; and with the mouth confession is made unto salvation.*

Baptism follows a verbal confession picturing a new life commitment to Christ as Savior and Lord. We are to make disciples. A disciple is a learner and follower of Christ. According to the Great Commission, all disciples are to be baptized.

The commission doesn't set forth two types of Christians. True believers are disciples. As disciples, they now have a new disposition. They desire to follow Jesus, and being raised to new life in Christ, they now have the power to follow Him.

Baptism doesn't save. But those who are saved desire to follow the Lord in baptism. It is an act of obedience, indicating the Christian is willing to live for Jesus. In baptism, we see the Ethiopian eunuch's commitment to follow the Lord. The eunuch was not only convinced and converted but he wanted to take the next step.

Local churches are to make disciples and baptism is the new

believer's opportunity to testify of his conversion. Likewise, as an ordinance administered by the local church, it is this testimony that joins them to a local church.

First and second century writings clearly demonstrate that the early church practiced believer's baptism. These writings reveal that those seeking baptism were first required—at a minimum—to make a verbal profession of faith in the Lord Jesus Christ.

Commenting on the significance of baptism in the early post-apostolic times, Ronald Heine states,

> One thing that is certainly obvious from these descriptions of baptism in the second-century church is that baptism was taken very seriously. It was not something entered into lightly by those who experienced it, nor was it something that was administered in an offhand way by the church. ***Baptism was considered … to mark a major break in a person's life. The person who entered into the water of baptism was making a major life commitment*** (emphasis added).[40]

Baptists have been willing to sacrifice and to pay the high price of persecution to obey the Lord in believer's immersion. David Cummins, in his unpublished notes on Baptist History, cites the following:

> Can you imagine gathering at an ice-covered creek in February and cutting a hole in the ice and descending into the icy water to observe the ordinance of baptism? And yet that is exactly what took place on that February day in 1794 when James Lemen, his wife, Catherine, and two others were '***buried in the likeness of His death***' at Fountaine Creek, in Monroe County, Illinois. These along with a few others, united in forming the first Baptist church in Illinois.[41]

---

[40] Ronald E. Heine, *Classical Christian Doctrine: Introducing the Essentials of the Ancient Faith* (Grand Rapids: Baker, 2013), 150-151.
[41] Edward P. Brand, *Illinois Baptists: A History* (Bloomington, IL: Pantagraph Printing Co., 1930), 24.

Cummins, in writing about the persecution of Baptists in Virginia, also recounts the following:

> For years in the Commonwealth of Virginia, Baptist preachers anticipated being so treated for preaching the Gospel without a license and for baptizing without state church authorization. We are reminded that prior to the Civil War, Baptist preachers were incarcerated in the Commonwealth of Virginia because they ministered without authorization from the state church. Personal animosity and prejudice often caused Baptist preachers to pay a severe price for their faithfulness. Elder John Tanner was an unusual man. He was imprisoned in Chesterfield, VA for daring to preach without state church authorization. He was not deterred, and when released he established a church in North Carolina. While in North Carolina he baptized Mrs. Dawson—a lady whose husband possessed a violent temper. Mr. Dawson had threatened to kill any man who baptized his wife. We are not able to ascertain whether Elder Tanner knew of that threat or not, but he had followed the will of God and had baptized Mrs. Dawson upon her profession of faith.
>
> The following June, Mr. Dawson learned that Elder Tanner would be preaching at the Sandy Run meeting house, and he made his way on the roadway and hid himself in the over growth. As Elder Tanner approached, Mr. Dawson fired upon him with a horseman's pistol and seventeen buckshot went into Elder Tanner's thigh. A doctor was immediately summoned, and Elder Tanner was carried to the house of Mr. Elisha Williams in Scotland Neck, North Carolina. In the course of time Elder Tanner recovered. The man of God never sought recompense but submitted to the suffering patiently as having been persecuted for Christ's sake.[42]

---

[42] Lewis Peyton Little, *Imprisoned Preachers and Religious Liberty in Virginia* (Lynchburg, VA: J. P. Bell Company, Inc., 1938), 337-338.

Our Baptist forefathers were beaten, abused, imprisoned, persecuted, and even shot for insisting on following the Lord's commandment—this ordinance of believer's immersion.

We are living in a day of hostility from the world and, sadly, great indifference in the churches. Many who profess to be saved never obey the Lord in baptism. Churches continue to lower the Biblical requirements of Christian commitment and, at the same time, wonder why membership numbers are falling and the power of God has departed.

For me, baptism was a significant event. I decided to follow Jesus—no turning back, no turning back!

What about infants and baptismal regeneration?

Baptismal regeneration is the belief that baptism is a physical means by which individuals obtain grace from God. This teaching is rooted in Augustinian Covenantalism. Many of this persuasion reason that "regeneration can take place in the smallest of infants... in the sphere of the covenant of God, He usually regenerates His elect children from infancy."[43]

Baptismal regeneration seems to have first appeared in the late second or early third century.[44] This heresy held that baptism removed the stain of original sin, leading ultimately to salvation. Others went further, arguing that baptism was equivalent to the new birth, securing regeneration.[45]

Many historical sources support that infant baptism emerged in conjunction with, and perhaps in response to, the development of the doctrine of baptismal regeneration.[46] For, if baptism affects regeneration which secures an individual's eternal salvation, then

---

[43] Hoeksema, *Reformed Dogmatics*, 464.

[44] Robert A. Baker and John M. Landers, *A Summary of Christian History* (Nashville: Broadman & Holman, 2005), eBook, 38.

[45] Baker and Landers, *Summary of Christian History*, 38.

[46] By the Council of Carthage in 252 AD these two doctrines were clearly wedded. See Thomas Armitage, *A History of the Baptists* (Watertown, WI: Roger Williams Heritage Archives, 1886), 161, 186-187.

each person should be baptized at the earliest opportunity. These heresies must be rejected.

Spurgeon spoke clearly to this issue:

> As long as you give baptism to an unregenerate child, people will imagine that it must do the child good. They will ask, 'If it does not do the child any good, why is it baptized?' The statement that it puts children into the covenant, or renders them members of the invisible church, is only a veiled form of the fundamental error of Baptismal Regeneration. If you keep up the ordinance, you will always have men superstitiously believing that some good comes to the baby thereby. And what is that but popery?
>
> I am amazed that an unconscious babe should be made the partaker of an ordinance which, according to the plain teaching of the Scriptures, requires the conscious and complete heart-trust of the recipient. Very few, if any, would argue that infants ought to receive the Lord's Supper. But there is no more scriptural warrant for bringing them to the one ordinance than there is for bringing them to the other.[47]

Historically, the mode of baptism and the subjects of baptism have been closely associated. Though the immersion of infants has been the continuous practice of the Greek church, the much larger Roman church used the pouring or sprinkling of infants. The Anabaptists opposed the baptizing of infants using either mode, but it is easy to see that the distortion of both the mode and subjects of baptism led to a perversion of the gospel.

The opposition of the Anabaptists is clearly seen in their writings. Infant baptism was called "the highest and chief abomination of the pope."[48] Menno Simons qualified infant baptism as a "human

---

[47] Charles Spurgeon, "Signs Of The Times", Metropolitan Tabernacle Pulpit, Vol. 19, S. No. 1135, Luke 12:54-57, delivered October 5, 1873.
[48] Placher, William C., *Readings in the History of Christian Theology: Vol. II* (Philadelphia: Westminster Press, 1988), 31.

invention, an opinion of men, a perversion of the ordinance of Christ."[49]

Clearly, the Reformers, intending to reform and not to separate from the Roman Church, never went far enough and were destined for future doctrinal deviations, having the seeds of compromise embedded in their movement. Anabaptists were persecuted and martyred by both Catholics and Protestants because the latter retained belief in the baptism of infants which conferred the power of regeneration into the family of God.

One of the arguments for the baptism of infants and very young children is that the Bible speaks of entire households being baptized. The assumption made is that infants must be included. But what does the Bible say about household baptisms? There is no reference to the baptism of infants in the New Testament.

The first case is the salvation of the first Gentiles, the household of Cornelius (Acts 10:43-48). Verse 43 speaks of believing to receive remission of sins. These Gentiles heard the word of God from Peter and apparently believed it because they received the Holy Spirit (44). The believing Jews were astonished but were convinced that God had saved these Gentiles (45).

In Acts 11, we have the record of Peter rehearsing the salvation of Cornelius's household. He describes this household as those "who believed on the Lord" (17). The Jews had previously believed and received the Holy Spirit; later these Gentiles also believed with the same confirming result. Water baptism could not be withheld without withstanding or opposing what God was accomplishing.

Lydia's faith in Christ is recorded in Acts 16:14-15. She was a seller of purple from the city of Thyatira. Somewhat humorously, Dr . David Cummins used to relate the following that he heard from Dr. Richard Clearwaters:

> Lydia, a business woman, ...came all the way to Philippi. Were there children too young in Lydia's household to believe? The

---

[49] Placher, *Readings*, 33.

term household may or may not include children. If we argue that Lydia's household included children, we must presume that Lydia was married, that Lydia had children, that Lydia's children were under the age of accountability, and that Lydia brought these children on her business trip on this long journey hundreds of miles by sea.[50]

Sometimes the word *household* refers to those of one's immediate family, but it may also include servants under the authority of their master. *The Baker Encyclopedia of the Bible* gives the following information of a *household* in Biblical times.

Persons who live in the same place and compose a family or extended family. In biblical times a household included father, mother(s), children, grandparents, servants, concubines, and sojourners. Jacob's household included 66 people, not counting the wives of his sons (Gen. 46:26). In the NT some entire households were baptized (Acts 11:14).[51]

In the case of Crispus and his household in Corinth, believing clearly preceded baptism (Acts 18:8). There's no mention of infants being included because they would be incapable of exercising personal faith. A reference to Paul's ministry or preaching the gospel in Corinth is found in his first letter to this church. In the context of declaring the priority of the gospel over baptism, Paul states that he baptized the household of Stephanas (1:16). He later commends this household for being "addicted to the ministry" (16:15). Those baptized of Stephanas' household were capable of local church ministry. They were not infants in the nursery!

The case of the Philippian Jailer provides a similar example in that all who were baptized had first heard and believed the word of the Lord. The whole house was baptized because the whole house

---

[50] From the notes of Dr. David Cummins.
[51] Walter A. Elwell, ed., "household," *The Baker Encyclopedia of the Bible* (Grand Rapids, MI: Baker Book House, 1988), Logos Bible Software Research Edition.

believed.

> *(Acts 16:32-34) And they **spake unto him the word of the Lord, and to all that were in his house**.... ³⁴**And when he had brought them into his house, he set meat** before them, and rejoiced, **believing in God with all his house**.*

Does baptism save?

The Reformers were, at best, unclear about the purpose and efficacy of baptism; their teachings, not unlike Reformed theologians today, are on a spectrum of misguided to the very heretical. Often, they seem to contradict their own writings and always mar the picture of conversion found in believer's immersion. John Calvin wrote,

> God in baptism promises remission of sins, and will undoubtedly perform what he has promised to all believers. That promise was ***offered to us in baptism***; let us therefore embrace it in faith (emphasis added).⁵²

And so, Calvin says remission of sins is offered in baptism and we must embrace it by faith, leaving one to ask, "Are we saved by faith or baptism or both?" At it's best, infant baptism creates theological fog. The Scripture is clear: we are saved through faith alone (Eph. 2:8).

While there are texts that may *seem* to make baptism a saving ordinance, none of these Scriptures would prescribe the mode of sprinkling or the baptism of infants by any mode.

The following text was considered at the end of chapter 2:

> *(1 Peter 3:21) The like figure whereunto even baptism doth also now save us (not the putting away of the filth of the flesh, but **the answer of a good conscience toward God**,) by the resurrection of Jesus Christ:*

Peter speaks of a conscience that has been cleansed from the defilement of sin. Baptism is the outward response to God's

---

⁵² White, *The Potter's Freedom*, 101.

cleansing by a resurrected, living Jesus Christ. The believer's baptism testifies to the reality of the Resurrection.

Another verse frequently used in attempting to support baptismal regeneration is Acts 2:38. Once again, adults are clearly the focus and there is no support for infant baptism. Being baptized "for the remission of sins" means "because of" or "on account of" or "in reference to" the remission of sins as a direct result of genuine repentance (Acts 2:38) and the reception of the word about Messiah Jesus (Acts 2:41). It is undisputed and significant that the baptism of converts came after repentance and faith.

On the other side of the discussion, there are those who deny baptism is for this dispensation, believing that it ceased to be commanded in the first century. One text used in support is written to the church in Corinth. Paul says that Christ did not send him to baptize.

> *(1 Corinthians 1:14-17) I thank God that I baptized none of you, but Crispus and Gaius; ¹⁵Lest any should say that I had baptized in mine own name. ¹⁶And I baptized also the household of Stephanas: besides, I know not whether I baptized any other. ¹⁷For* **Christ sent me not to baptize, but to preach the gospel**: *not with wisdom of words, lest the cross of Christ should be made of none effect.*

But the text teaches that baptism and the gospel are distinct. Baptism is not part of the gospel; the text has the gospel and baptism in contrast. Baptism only attests to the fact that a person has believed the gospel and received newness of life.

However, Paul is not saying that baptisms are unimportant and should not be performed. He is declaring the first importance, the priority of the gospel (1 Cor. 15:1). The content of the gospel is described as the death, burial, and resurrection of Jesus Christ with no inclusion of baptism (15:3). Notice a similar verse from the New Testament that uses the lesser to emphasize the priority and importance of the greater. Matthew is quoting Hosea 6:6.

> *(Matthew 9:13) But go ye and learn what that meaneth,* **I will**

have mercy, and not sacrifice: for I am not come to call the righteous, but sinners to repentance.

There are many verses in the Old Testament. which commanded sacrifice. Does the Bible contradict itself? No. The writer, quoting God's words, is using a comparative as a figure of speech. This is not to be taken in the absolute sense. God required many sacrifices, but obedience was much more important. Baptism is important; but preaching the gospel is much more important than baptism. To this every true believer can say, "Amen!"

Baptism is a prerequisite to church membership.

We clearly see from the order of the Great Commission found in Matthew 28:18-20 that a person must first believe or become a disciple, and then be baptized, before being taught to do all things commanded by Christ.

This was the pattern practiced by the early church. Baptism was considered the first step of obedience to Christ after conversion. Baptism always followed conversion and is never considered to have saving power. Therefore, the only proper subject for baptism is a person who has professed faith in Christ for salvation (Acts 2:42; 8:27-40; 10:44-48; Acts 16:31-33). As such, baptism is a prerequisite to church membership (Acts 2:41-43).

It appears that in early church practice being added to the church was after baptism but an immediate outcome of baptism. There is immediate association with the local church so that it could not be said that it is necessary to make a separate decision about membership (Acts 2:41).

At Pentecost, Peter commanded the hearers to repent and be baptized (Acts 2:38). Three thousand hearers **believed**, were **baptized**, and **belonged** to the church. This description becomes a prescription as we observe the practice of the early church. The normal pattern in Acts is that believers were baptized and immediately added to the membership of a local church. The early church practiced regenerate, immersed church membership.

The proper authority for baptism is the local church.

Who is to baptize converts? The command to baptize disciples (Mat. 28:19) was given to the apostles who became the foundation of the local church (Eph. 2:20).

Baptism is a church ordinance. The practice of the Lord's Supper assumes church association for the participants with the words, "when ye come together in the church" (1 Corinthians 11:18; also 20,33,34). Those who come together in the body are identified by their public testimony of faith in Christ through baptism (1 Cor. 12:13).

Acts records that believers were baptized and added to the membership of a local church or that they became part of a new church upon their baptism. Believers were baptized in Samaria (Acts 8:5-12). After the fact, we are told that churches were established in that region (Acts 9:31). Phillip apparently acted on the authority of the church at Jerusalem when he baptized the converts in Samaria and when he baptized the Ethiopian eunuch (Acts 8:38).

The proper administrator is then whoever is designated by the local church.

According to Hiscox,

> Baptism is usually administered by ordained *ministers*. And this is proper, regular, and orderly. But should occasion require, and the church so direct, it would be equally valid if administered by a deacon or any private member selected for that service. The validity depends on the character and profession of the candidate, and not on that of the administrator. As to the qualifications of administrators, the New Testament is silent, except that they were disciples.[53]

Since this ordinance signifies the beginning of a local church

---

[53] Edward T. Hiscox: *The New Directory for Baptist Churches, 1962 edition* (Valley Forge, PA: The Judson Press, 1894), 129.

relationship, questions remain: "What constitutes valid baptism?" And another follows: "Should a believer be rebaptized when transferring his membership from one local church to another?"

Believer's baptism is not normally repeated upon a believer's transfer to another local church. Since rebaptism violates the picture of a once-for-all time salvation, it may be as wrong to be rebaptized as it is to refuse or neglect baptism altogether.

It should not be required of anyone to be baptized again if he or she had been immersed after confession of faith in Christ. This would be true in all cases except when the baptism was received through a church which perverts the gospel. In a sense, rebaptism in cases like these would be a repudiation of the heretical doctrine of the previous church.

When I planted and pastored an independent Baptist church in the south, I learned that there are convention Baptists who will not accept the baptism of a person coming from a church outside their denomination. On one occasion, an entire family who was saved and baptized in our church, after being members for a few years, attempted to join one of the convention churches. However, to accept the family for membership, the church required them first to be rebaptized. When the husband protested, the pastor suggested that the family join a theologically liberal convention church which would accept anyone's baptism. Then, he said they could transfer the family to their church without rebaptism because they would be coming from another convention church. As absurd as this is, to be fair, there are some independents who refuse to recognize the baptisms of convention churches or even those of certain other independent Baptists. The recognition of a valid baptism should never be made with respect to a church's secondary practices.

In contrast, Bible-believing churches should never receive people who have been baptized in cults like Mormonism, the Jehovah's Witnesses, or Adventism. These are heretical cults, and their baptism is invalid because the religious sect preaches a perverted gospel. Likewise, the immersion of a true believer from a church which practices baptismal regeneration or from certain charismatic groups should not be accepted as valid. These groups also preach a perversion of the gospel. Baptism from any group that promotes baptismal regeneration should be rejected. In cases like these, believers should be baptized to identify with the truth of the gospel and a church that teaches the same.

The Lord has commanded both the church to baptize believers and for believers to be baptized. Both the church and the individual believer have specific responsibilities. According to Matthew 28:18-20, those who become disciples are to be baptized. The church has the responsibility to examine the testimony of every professing convert. "It is not only important that men be saved before baptism, but it is vital that men be baptized after being saved!"[54]

---

[54] Paul R. Jackson, *The Doctrine and Administration of the Church* (Des Plaines, IL: Regular Baptist Press, 1968), 65.

5

The Ordinances Teach Us
about The Church (Part 2)

The Lord's Supper stresses local church fellowship.

The baptism of believers is a church ordinance. It not only pictures a believer's conversion, but it publicly associates them with the local church of fellow believers. In a similar way, the Lord's Supper identifies members of the church. In the longest passage in the New Testament concerning the practice of the Lord's Supper (1 Cor. 11:17–34), church association is assumed using the words, "when ye come together in the church" (1 Cor. 11:18; also 20,33,34).

Paul begins his comments on the Lord's Supper saying, "...there are divisions among you, and in part I believe it" (1 Cor. 11:18). He may be connecting their practice of the Lord's Supper to the divisions noted in the early part of the letter (1:10). The word *"divisions"* (*schismata*) is used in both places. Or, he may be making a more comprehensive statement about their poor relationships, as well as specific conduct while celebrating the Supper. Whatever the broader context, the Corinthian church was guilty of creating social divisions in the church, separating the rich from the poor.

The Purpose of the Lord's Supper

Communion is a time when the church "comes together." The Love Feast was a meal eaten prior to partaking of the elements of communion where the members would bring food and eat together. Its purpose was to demonstrate oneness and promote fellowship among the members.

In assembling for the Lord's Supper, the church is declaring its "one bread" (10:17) unity in Christ and the resulting fellowship with one another. This is why the Apostle Paul treats the matter of divisions among the church so seriously. The church's conduct was contrary to the truth of the gospel. The gospel elevates all believers to a standing of common ground in Christ. There are no favorites at the Lord's Table. Therefore, anything that promotes exclusivity or distinguishes believers as superior or inferior by worldly standards is rendered irrelevant by the truth of the gospel.

Rather than picturing the common salvation in Christ enjoyed by all members of the church—rich and poor, slave and master, male and female, Jew and Gentile—what they are proclaiming is the ongoing observance of class distinctions in the church. Paul understands the behavior of "those who have" to be such that it both despises the church and shames "those who have not."[55]

> (Galatians 3:28) There is neither Jew nor Greek, there is neither bond nor free, there is neither male nor female: for ye are all one in Christ Jesus.

---

[55] James M. Hamilton Jr., "The Lord's Supper In Paul: An Identity-Forming Proclamation Of The Gospel," 2010, http://jimhamilton.info/wp-content/uploads/2010/12/lords-supper-in-paul-formtted.pdf.

The gospel calls all without distinction as to race, gender, or class. The church brings them all together as one in Christ. By their behavior, the Corinthian church was declaring a distorted gospel which regards wealth and status as virtuous pursuits.

The Problems at the Lord's Supper

The abuses surrounding the Lord's Supper were severe to the point that the Apostle rebuked the Corinthians, saying that their meal was not the Lord's. In other words, their eating together does not display the characteristics the Lord intended. Presumably to avoid sharing what they had with those less fortunate, some arrived before the entire church assembled and ate privately. As the context shows, their conduct was divisive, selfish, uncharitable, and even demeaning toward others. This is not the *Lord's* supper.

> *(1 Corinthians 11:20) When ye come together therefore into one place, this is not to eat the Lord's supper.*

The Lord's Supper is designed to be a testimony to the work of Christ. His sacrificial death not only provided for the salvation of believing sinners of all mankind, but His death also reconciled all believers into His body, beginning with breaking down the greatest division, that of Jews and Gentiles. The Corinthian church had missed the purpose of the love feast, which was to demonstrate their love and unity in Jesus Christ by eating together.

> *(1 Corinthians 11:17) Now in this that I declare unto you I praise you not, that ye come together not for the better, but for the worse.*

If the church's coming together was truly in recognition and celebration of this unity provided by Christ, their meeting would have been for the "better." But rather than this positive purpose being fulfilled, their meeting was a negative experience; it was for the "worse" because their action marred the picture of Christ bringing redeemed sinners into fellowship with Him and with one another in the local church. Their coming together did not strengthen fellowship in the church; it weakened relationships and communicated division.

> *(1 Corinthians 11:19) For there must be also heresies among you, that they which are approved may be made manifest among you.*

The word *heresies* means *factions*. The Greek word suggests an exclusionary preference for one group over another. In other words, the wealthy Corinthians were cliquish. They excluded the poor from their circle of fellowship. The poor were not denied access to the church, to the meal, or the Supper, but they were excluded from fellowship between brothers and sisters in Christ in the truest sense.

This word is one of the works of the flesh listed in Galatians 5:20. Factious persons are not Spirit-controlled and are out of step with the purposes of God pictured in the Lord's Supper. Instead of putting others before themselves, they acted selfishly.

> *(1 Corinthians 11:21) For in eating every one **taketh before other** (**goes ahead**, ESV) his own supper: and one is hungry, and another is drunken.*

Rather than bringing food to share with the poor, the rich would arrive early and consume their food before the poor showed up. Consequently, the poor went home hungry. Their selfish actions were inconsistent with the impartiality of God's love (Acts 10:34) as well as the unity of the body of Christ, the church (1 Cor. 12:13-14,20).

> *(1 Corinthians 11:22) What? have ye not houses to eat and to drink in? or despise ye the church of God, and shame them that have not? What shall I say to you? shall I praise you in this? I praise you not.*

Some churches have wrongly interpreted this question thinking that Paul is saying it is wrong to have a church dinner. Or others say that food shouldn't be eaten in the church building.

Paul was not saying that it was wrong to eat in church or at church, but he was saying that they had destroyed the meaning of the Love Feast. Instead of recognizing a spiritual purpose in their gathering, they made the meal all about their own satisfaction. In an appeal to their consciences, the Apostle asks the probing question: "have ye not houses to eat and to drink in?" If this meal is only about a physical meal, then you can do that in your own house!

It is best to understand the charge of despising the church of God (11:22b) as acting contrary to the purpose intended for the church, and thereby conducting themselves in opposition to God Himself. Some have suggested sarcasm in Paul's words here, but this is a charge of serious consequence. The actions of the rich and aloof, if continued without correction, could lead to the demise of this local church.

There are no big people or little people in the local church. Wealth, educational attainments, positions, titles, ethnicity, or any other human attributes or achievements are irrelevant to fellowship in the church. All members are sinners saved by grace. All are brothers and sisters in Christ.

They came together to remember Christ's sacrifice by which they were redeemed and made one, but their actions brought shame or humiliation to the poor (11:22c). Rather than displaying unconditional love and unity, they acted with selfish insensitivity to others. Their conduct opposed the very purpose of their gathering.

Yet, considering the many problems addressed in this letter, it is likely that their conduct at the feast and table were simply reflections of their overall defective relationships; sadly, it doubtless represented how they viewed and treated others on a regular basis.

The Psalmist captures the spirit that ought to prevail among brethren:

> (Psalm 133:1-3) Behold, how good and how pleasant it is for brethren to dwell together in unity! ²It is like the precious

ointment upon the head, that ran down upon the beard, even Aaron's beard: that went down to the skirts of his garments; ³As the dew of Hermon, and as the dew that descended upon the mountains of Zion: for there the LORD commanded the blessing, even life for evermore.

The Proper Participants at the Lord's Supper

There is debate among Baptists concerning who should be permitted to participate in the communion service in a local church. There is general agreement that those who are considered under church discipline are excluded. There are three views commonly held regarding all others.

Open communion

When a church invites professing believers in Christ to the Lord's Table regardless of when and how they were baptized, this church is practicing open communion. In the light of the purposes of communion previously cited, this view seems scripturally suspect.

The inconsistency of requiring immersion for church membership and not for the Lord's Supper is identified by H. L. Gear:

> We... see clearly the inconsistency in which all "open communion" Baptists are involved. They adopt the principle that baptism is prerequisite to church membership, but deny that it is prerequisite to the Lord's Supper. Holding that immersion is the only baptism, they will not suffer a Pedobaptist to join their church; or allow sprinkling, or pouring, or infant baptism to be practiced in their church; yet they will invite those who practice them to sit with them at the Lord's Table. But if they admit unbaptized persons and heretical departers from the truth to this ordinance, **which is the principal act and chief privilege of church fellowship**, on what principle of consistency can they deny them the right to participate in the other and lesser duties of church fellowship?[56]

---

[56] H. L. Gear, *The Relation of Baptism to the Lord's Supper* (Watertown, WI: Roger Williams Heritage Archives, 1880), 30–33.

Gear asserts that the Lord's Supper is the highest privilege of church fellowship. He is correct in that it symbolizes our common standing in Christ and our mutual care for one another. To allow someone to observe the picture which reminds the church of spiritual realities but disallow them to participate in church membership and local church service, is contradictory. Gear continues:

> On what principle do they say to the Pedobaptist, "You may sit at the Lord's Table with us without being baptized; but you cannot vote with us until you are baptized"? This mingling of "open communion" and close fellowship is like the mingling of oil and water; they cannot consistently go together. Nothing can be plainer than that, on the "open communion" principle, no Baptist church has any logical foundation on which to stand. *If baptism is not prerequisite to the Lord's Supper, it is prerequisite to nothing pertaining to the church*, and we have no right nor power to insist upon its observance. In that view, we should be bound by consistency to say to all: "Take your choice; be immersed, or be sprinkled, or let water be poured upon you, or let the whole matter alone, just as you please! Baptism is prerequisite to nothing! *Come and join us in church fellowship, and disobey Christ about baptism! We have no power to hold you accountable!*" Thus would Christ's ordinance be subverted, and his truth sold. It is just to this position that the "open communion" heresy would logically lead us (emphasis added).[57]

Gear was right, of course. The practice of open communion will logically lead to open membership. This term describes a church that does not require believer's immersion for membership.

The case of the infamous pastor of Park Avenue Baptist Church in New York City, Harry Emerson Fosdick, who became a central figure in the Fundamentalist-Modernist controversy in the 1920s, is instructive. His name became synonymous with compromise

---

[57] Gear, *The Relation of Baptism*, 30-33.

and theological liberalism. Fosdick was ordained as a Baptist but soon was called to First Presbyterian Church and concluded his ministry in the ecumenical, non-denominational Riverside Church in northwestern Manhattan.[58]

Caleb Morell cites Fosdick who advocated for open membership:

> If I had my way baptism would be altogether an individual affair. Anyone who wanted to be immersed, I would gladly immerse. Anyone who wanted to be sprinkled, I would glad [sic] sprinkle. If anyone was a Quaker and had conscientious scruples against any ritual, I would gladly without baptism welcome him on confession of faith. Why not?[59]

Baptists throughout history have been known for their insistence on believer's baptism by immersion. Neither because of some group consensus nor for the sake of denominational control, but because the Bible teaches it. Baptists are committed to obey whatever is taught in holy Scripture. Nothing can be left to individual conscience that is clearly contrary to the teaching of the word of God.

Morell rightly observes:

> …"open membership" was not simply a matter of arcane polity. They understood that in a Convention, as in a local church, opening membership to unbaptized persons was a step toward handing control over to those who may very well not be Christians, effectively mingling the church with the world.[60]

---

[58] "Harry Emerson Fosdick," *Wikipedia*. Accessed January 19, 2024. https://en.wikipedia.org/wiki/Harry_Emerson_Fosdick.
[59] Caleb Morell, "How Harry Emerson Fosdick's 'Open Membership' Overtook the Northern Baptist Convention." 9Marks, August 1, 2022. https://www.9marks.org/article/how-harry-emerson-fosdicks-open-membership-overtook-the-northern-baptist-convention/.
[60] Morell, "Harry Emerson Fosdick's 'Open Membership'."

Closed communion

Closed communion limits participation at the Lord's Table to those who are members in good standing of their own local church. This practice is supported by the obligations of accountability and responsibility of the members to their pastors and to the whole church. The gathered church members are picturing their local church unity and their submission to the church and Christ's under-shepherds. Those who belong to another local church have no accountability to the leadership of a church they may be visiting. Similarly, they do not have the same degree of responsibility to the members of another local church; however, they do have the responsibility of general Christian love to all believers, especially to those in churches of like faith and practice.

It is the right of a local church to limit the Lord's Supper to its own members. However, the right of decision does not ever justify an action. The local church is always responsible to conduct itself according to Biblical commands and principles. For example, the church determines the candidates they will baptize and the members they receive, but the church would be in error to exclude anyone based upon anything other than Christian testimony. Though open communion is clearly not supported in Scripture, and closed communion has some logical and Biblical support, there is another position that best fits the Biblical pattern.

Close communion

Practicing close communion means the church invites believers from other churches who are saved, scripturally immersed, and living in fellowship with God to their observance of the Lord's Supper. This practice only differs from closed communion in the exception made for those visiting on a temporary basis. The invitation is for members in good standing of churches of like faith to participate.

The New Testament emphasis is on local churches and sets forth these churches as independent and autonomous. However, there is clearly an interdependence among the churches taught in Scripture. Paul participated in observing the Lord's Supper in other churches, though he was not a member of those churches. He did so in Troas, yet he was only in that city for seven days. In comparing the phrase "the bread which we break" (1 Cor. 10:16) with the words "break bread" (Act 20:7), these words are clearly a reference to the Lord's Supper. The breaking of bread, or the Lord's Supper, was for the disciples which would have also included Paul (Mat. 28:19).

When Paul wrote "the bread which we break" (1 Cor. 10:16), he may have been alluding to his time in Corinth when he would have celebrated the Lord's Supper with the church. Certainly, he states as much as he begins to rehearse what he delivered to them from the Lord (11:23). Paul delivered the truth of the Lord's Supper to them. The account in Acts says he was with them 18 months (Acts 18:11).

The practice of open communion fails to meet scriptural requirements. It allows professing believers to continue in disobedience regarding baptism and possibly church membership as well. To participate in the Lord's Supper before being scripturally immersed communicates that one can enjoy church fellowship without the church commitment of membership. It is inconsistent to partake of the symbol of church fellowship without church association.

Since the Lord's Supper is a local church ordinance, and since baptism is a requirement for church membership, only saved and baptized persons should participate in the communion.

Closed communion meets the biblical requirements in all but the matter of the interdependence of churches and the shared fellowship of obedient brethren. In recognition of these principles and the practice of the Apostle Paul, close communion seems to best fit the New Testament pattern.

What additional requirements might there be for participation in the Lord's Supper in a New Testament Baptist church? The main qualification is an obedient walk. Paul commanded the Corinthian believers to ban professing Christians from the Lord's Table who were practicing a sinful lifestyle (1 Cor. 5:9-12) and he rebuked the Corinthian believers for their unholy and "unworthy" (1 Cor. 11:27-32) conduct at the communion table.

The purity of the church is one focus of the observance. Not only are believers to examine themselves but the church is to take the necessary steps of discipline regarding those who openly violate moral imperatives. In chapter five, Paul calls the Corinthian church to "celebrate the feast not in the old leaven" (1 Cor. 5:8), calling the church to cleanse itself from the one who has indulged in the "leaven" of sexual immorality (5:1–2).[61]

They would be excluded from the Lord's Table because they were excluded from the church! In the case of the Corinthian fornicator, he was engaged in scandalous, unrepentant public sin. At the time, the genuineness of his conversion was in doubt, though in the second epistle to the church, Paul celebrates both the church's actions and the repentance of the offender.

An interesting example of the importance of having standards for communion in the church was in the news regarding President Joe Biden. Though the Roman Catholic Mass is a heretical distortion of the Lord's Supper, the Church understands the necessity of guarding the participation and only allowing those in good standing to partake. In the context of the Roman Catholic Church denying the Eucharist to the president of the United States, we read:

> Apparently, Democrats are under the impression that communion is just a free-for-all, whereby the church can have no standards whatsoever in administering it. ... you don't even have to be Catholic to see how dumb this is. Protestants have different beliefs about communion, but they still follow the

---

[61] Hamilton, "The Lord's Supper In Paul."

Biblical decree to examine one's self and to make sure that one is worthy of taking it. Paul is pretty clear that if you aren't, you are sinning against the Body of Christ.[62]

The Precautions in the Lord's Supper

A believer in Christ can't be in fellowship with God's people unless he is living in fellowship with God.

In verses 17-22, Paul rebukes the Corinthian church for drunkenness while coming together for a meal prior to the Lord's Supper, as well as for divisions and shameful conduct toward less fortunate members.

Verses 23-26 rehearses the Lord's Supper as it was given by the Lord Jesus and communicated through Paul. By understanding the meaning and by obeying the teachings pictured in the Lord's Supper, we are prepared to properly relate to our fellow members in the church.

After laying this foundation, the Apostle offers both warnings and correctives (1 Cor. 11:27-34). There are severe consequences for mistreatment of Christ's own children, His redeemed, who are brothers and sisters in the local church.

> *(1 Corinthians 11:27) Wherefore whosoever shall eat this bread, and drink this cup of the Lord, **unworthily**, shall be guilty of the body and blood of the Lord.*

It is possible to observe the Lord's Supper "unworthily" by either coming in an irreverent or in an improper way. The text doesn't specify the particulars of unworthy eating, but the context and the nature of the Supper suggest some warnings. The context of eating is in the Lord's church and the nature of the Supper is one belonging to the Lord. The Corinthians were coming to the Supper in an unworthy manner by their disregard for their brethren and

---

[62] Bonchie, "Democrats Go to War." with the Catholic Church," RedState.com, June 18, 2021, https://redstate.com/bonchie/2021/06/18/democrats-go-to-war-with-the-catholic-church-n398957.

by their careless conduct. Some were even drunken (compare 1 Cor 11:21) through the prior consumption of wine during the Love Feast.

Not only were the Corinthians partaking of Communion in an unworthy manner by disrespecting fellow believers, but also by a lack of reverence for the Lord; this Supper is the Lord's. This is not an ordinary meal; this is not common eating and drinking. Treating the Lord's Supper, and the shared meal leading to it, in a cavalier way brings both the displeasure and discipline of God. This is not a time to party with friends, but an opportunity to share with church family.

The purpose of the Lord's Supper is to picture the fellowship of the believer with the Lord and the fellowship of believers in the church. Fellowship is based upon repentant faith in the person and work of Jesus Christ which is remembered through the bread and cup. The Supper is for those who are living in fellowship with Christ, living by faith as pictured in eating the bread and confessing sin as drinking the cup testifies.

Certainly no one lives without sin; this truth is symbolized in the often-repeated partaking of the cup. As a believer walks with the Lord, he will periodically stumble, and he must confess his sin to restore fellowship with the Lord. The Lord is faithful and just in forgiving the believer's sin (1 John 1:9). A believer should never participate in the Lord's Supper with unconfessed sin in his life. If a Christian is unwilling to obey the Lord, then he is not living in fellowship. This person must first repent and seek the forgiveness of God before partaking of the Supper.

The passage establishes the need for being rightly related to others in the church. The case of the Corinthians establishes the principle of care for brothers and sisters in Christ. If slighting brethren at the communion meal is rebuked, then the greater matters of sin causing bitterness and broken fellowship must be addressed. Confession, forgiveness and reconciliation between believers are necessary preparations for Communion.

Certainly, the most basic qualification for sharing in the Lord's Supper is to be a genuine believer. In a sense, the Lord's Supper becomes a repeated evangelistic appeal to those who have made a profession of faith in Christ and to those who may observe believers celebrating together. Those who participate are proclaiming by their actions that they have believed, know God, and are safe in Jesus Christ. An unbeliever places themselves in a dangerous place of possible self-deception as well as being shielded from the evangelistic efforts of true believers. This would make this person "guilty of the body and blood of the Lord" on the most basic level. This would be denial of the purpose and value of God's provision in Christ, as well as a statement of self-righteousness. Treating the elements representing Christ's unique life and death as something common and insignificant brings dishonor to Christ Himself.

The warning of unworthy eating calls for self-examination (11:28).

(1 Corinthians 11:28) But let a man examine himself, and so let him eat of that bread, and drink of that cup.

There should be a personal examination before the eating of the Lord's Supper. Not until we have examined ourselves and dealt with any sin or improper motive, is anyone ready to share in the bread and the cup. Those who eat and drink "unworthily" are subject to the discipline of God for failure in "discerning" the Lord's body (11:29).

(1 Corinthians 11:29) For he that eateth and drinketh unworthily, eateth and drinketh damnation to himself, not discerning the Lord's body.

To eat and drink unworthily means to eat in a manner that does not conform to the purpose of the Supper. The following explanation of this meaning is based upon references to Christian living.

The adverb ἀναξίως (*anaxiōs*, unworthily) refers to doing something that does not square with the character or nature of something (cf. Eph. 4:1; Phil. 1:27; Col. 1:10; 1 Thess. 2:12). Here they are partaking in a manner that violates the purpose to proclaim the Lord's death.[63]

For example, for a believer to "walk worthy" (Eph. 4:1) is to live a life consistent with one's profession of faith; it is to live to properly reflect the work of Christ. In the case of the Ephesians, it involved showing humility and longsuffering toward fellow-Christians. This is a positive admonition, while a similar warning is stated negatively to the Corinthians. Those partaking "unworthily" would bring judgment to themselves. The Greek word translated *damnation* is better translated *judgment* as in the NKJV. It refers to the Lord's discipline of believers, not the damnation of unbelievers.

There are two legitimate views on what Paul is teaching in regard to "discerning the Lord's body." First, he may be referring to the elements representing Christ's physical body which were given for us (10:16; 11:27). The believer who fails to discern the Lord's body, that is, the proper meaning and application of His life and death, will experience the chastening of the Lord. They will be judged for not discerning the Lord's body, for not recognizing implications of the person and work of Jesus Christ. This understanding makes the Supper different than any other meal and the conduct of believers should reflect its holy nature.

The second view seems more likely. Beginning in verse 23, Paul gives the "for" or reason why the church should be inclusive of all members and not respect class or economic distinctions. The Lord's Supper speaks to the work of Christ for all. Believers share a mutual faith and an equal standing in Christ. And so, in rebuking the Corinthian church for its treatment of the poor among them, Paul is likely moving back to his main theme and is speaking of "the body" in reference to the Lord's church (10:17). Truly, the Lord Jesus gave his body and blood to redeem sinners, but He also did so to establish a new body called the church.

---

[63] David E. Garland, *First Corinthians, Baker Exegetical Commentary on the New Testament* (Grand Rapids, MI: Baker Academic, 2003), 550–555.

(1 Corinthians 10:16-17) The cup of blessing which we bless, is it not the communion of the blood of Christ? The bread which we break, is it not the communion of the body of Christ? [17]For we being many are one bread, and one body: for we are all partakers of that one bread.

If the reference is to the church as the Lord's body, then the believers are being warned to recognize that we share a mutual identity and belong to one another. We do not live our Christian lives in isolation. Jesus established the church, and we live in communion with Him and with His people. Therefore, it is important to "tarry" or wait for one another (11:33).

These possible interpretations are very compatible. In either case, the demands are similar. Both are calling for love and unity in the church.

A proper understanding of what these elements represent should change the Corinthians' attitude and behavior toward others. It reminds them of their dependence on Christ and their own interdependence and should cause them to share their own provisions with others at the meal who have little or nothing.[64]

If one sees the "Lord's body" as a specific application to the Corinthian problem of disrespecting unfortunate members, then the warning about partaking unworthily would relate primarily to one's personal fellowship with the Lord and would apply, but not be limited, to relationships in the church.

The Corinthians were already suffering the consequences of their misbehavior. Paul probably has heard of these deaths from the same ones who told him of their divisions, and he connects these events to their improper handling of the sacred Lord's Supper and to God's judgment (cf. 10:4–5).[65]

(1 Corinthians 11:30) For this cause many are weak and sickly among you, and many sleep.

---

[64] Garland, *1 Corinthians*, 550–555.
[65] Ibid.

"For this cause," because of their improper conduct when coming together for the Lord's Supper, many of them had suffered the chastisement of God. Some became sick and others died. These were caused by the direct intervention of God. The Lord disciplined the Corinthians' abuse of the Lord's Supper by causing some to be sick and taking the lives of others. There is no spiritualizing here; this is real sickness and real death. The word "weak" speaks of a condition where one is worn down or debilitated. The word *sickly* speaks of those without good health. The word *sleep* is a common New Testament metaphor for the death of believers (John 11:11; Acts 7:60; 1 Thess. 4:13-15). Many had died because of how they had treated the Lord's Supper and their fellow believers in Christ.

The Apostle turns to remedy and hope. God's chastisement may be prevented if we would first examine ourselves, seek forgiveness, and take necessary corrections.

> *(1 Corinthians 11:31) For if we would judge ourselves, we should not be judged.*

The believer's self-judgment will avert God's judgment. God disciplines His children to correct their sinful behavior and direct them in the paths of righteousness. However, the text warns that failure to correct one's behavior may result in physical death. But God's redeemed children are under the discipline of their Heavenly Father, which prevents them from ever being condemned with the world. There is no condemnation to those in Christ Jesus and no separation from the love of Christ (Rom. 8:1,35). No believer should fear losing his salvation or being eternally separated from the presence of God.

> *(1 Corinthians 11:32) But when we are judged, we are chastened of the Lord, that we should not be condemned with the world.*

To summarize, individual believers are to take the initiative to deal with personal sin that would break fellowship with God or fellow believers. If they do, the Lord will not judge them. But if not, the Lord will take the initiative and do the judging. And His discipline may at times be severe.

In verses 33 and 34 the Apostle again emphasizes the need for proper conduct toward our brethren. The members are to "tarry" or wait for one another.

> *(1 Corinthians 11:33-34) Wherefore, my brethren, when ye come together to eat, tarry one for another. [34]And if any man hunger, let him eat at home; that ye come not together unto condemnation. And the rest will I set in order when I come.*

Christ died for our brethren as well as for us; they are equally the objects of the love of God. They have equal standing before Him and deserve equal treatment by the brethren around the Table. In fact, through the example of our Lord, they ought to receive priority treatment. As the Lord Jesus washed the disciples' feet and became a servant to all, ultimately demonstrating His love for us on the cross, we ought to come to the Table giving rather than taking. Christ's death for us not only pays for our sin, it also leaves us an example for giving of ourselves and preferring others over ourselves. Because they are loved by God and belong to Him through Christ, we must respect other believers as the Lord's property. One cannot be right with the Lord, if he is not right with his brother or sister in Christ.

The command to wait or tarry doesn't mean to simply delay the eating until all are present. The problem was a selfish lack of sharing and perhaps a snobbishness that caused those with much to avoid eating with the less fortunate. To wait and then eat alone without sharing isn't what Paul had in mind. They were to wait in order to share with those who may otherwise go hungry (11:21).

The idea of eating at home to satisfy hunger doesn't mean that no eating was to take place at the assembly. The purpose of the gathering for the Lord's Supper is the emphasis of the command. Coming together was for the purpose of fellowship, sharing the common faith, and demonstrating the unity of all believers in the church. Staying home would not relieve any of them from this responsibility. The Lord commanded, "This do..." The Lord's

Supper is not optional; it is a call to remember Christ and to follow Him as members of the local church.

6

The Ordinances Identify Church Members and Guide Church Practices

The ordinances define the local church: its membership and practices.

The Ordinances Identify Local Church Members

Baptism defines the local church membership. Through baptism believers are added to the church. Prior to baptism and its accompanying testimony, the professing believer is not admitted into church fellowship.

As we have repeatedly emphasized, Acts 2:41-42 gives the biblical pattern. As believers are baptized, they are "added" to the church. This pattern was followed daily in the days right after Pentecost (Acts 2:47).

Baptism and church membership are not just individual decisions. It is truly the decision of the individual to receive Christ and no one else can decide this for them. The individual must decide to be baptized but the church must decide to recognize their testimony as one consistent with the word of God. The church examines the testimony of those who profess Christ and who seek identity with His people. When the local church baptizes, they are publicly identifying with the subject and receiving them into the care of the body.

Newly baptized believers are not simply added to a list or membership role; they are really "added" to serve and to be served. They become indispensable members of the church body giving and receiving mutual care as well as being accountable in their Christian conduct. Pastors are given the responsibility of caring for the sheep (1 Peter 5:2) and watching for the souls (Hebrews 13:17) of those under their charge. Church membership identifies the subjects of their responsibilities.

Local church members are also identified at the Lord's Table. By participation, they are saying they belong to the Lord and are in fellowship with the church's members.

Not only is a participant acknowledging identification with Christ and submission to His will, but also is declaring his commitment to care for fellow members. While baptism is a testimony of justification and the believer's initial repentant faith in Jesus Christ, the Lord's Supper pictures the Lord's sanctifying work and the believer's ongoing obedience to the will of Jesus Christ. The Lord's will would include involvement in every duty of local church life, including participation in church worship, submission to church leadership, care of its members, as well as the church's testimony to the world.

The church also has responsibility to invite only scripturally qualified believers to participate in the ordinances. Openly or publicly disobedient believers must be excluded from the Lord's Supper observance as well as the fellowship meal proceeding it (1 Cor. 5:11).

The following Scriptures speak of separating from anyone who claims to be brother in Christ but is living in open, unrepentant sin. The previous verses deal with the commands concerning the very scandalous fornication being committed by a professing believer in the Corinthian church (1 Cor. 5:1).

> *(1 Corinthians 5:7-13) Purge out therefore the old leaven, that ye may be a new lump, as ye are unleavened.... [9]I wrote unto you in an epistle not to company with fornicators: [10]Yet not altogether with the fornicators of this world, or with the covetous, or extortioners, or with idolaters; for then must ye needs go out of the world. [11]But now I have written unto you not to keep company, if any man that is called a brother be a fornicator, or covetous, or an idolater, or a railer, or a drunkard, or an extortioner;* ***with such an one no not to eat.*** *[12]For what have I to do to judge them also that are without? do not ye judge them that are within? [13]But them that are without God judgeth. Therefore put away from among yourselves that wicked person.*

The church is instructed "not to eat" with anyone who is living in open sin. The testimony of Christ to those on the outside of the church is being compromised by brazen sinful conduct. These should be "put away" rather than welcomed warmly to the fellowship of the Lord's Table.

Fortunately, cases requiring church discipline and exclusion from the Lord's Supper are usually few. But the church needs to be warned of the dangers of private sins as well. Those who are not confessing personal sin, and as such are denying the picture of the cup, should be warned not to partake. Likewise, those who are disobedient to the word of God are not presently walking by faith. Their partaking of the bread, as the symbol of obedient faith, would be inconsistent with the meaning of the ordinance. Sin that is unknown to others is always known by God. Self-examination and repentance are required before partaking of the Supper.

Both baptism and the Lord's Supper call for a resolve to follow Jesus Christ with no turning back, whatever the cost. Baptism is an open declaration of the believer's faith in Christ. Participating in the Lord's Supper communicates this same ongoing faith to the other members of the church. Partaking of the ordinances communicates to the church our testimony of belonging to Jesus

Christ and living to please Him.

The Ordinances Guide Local Church Practices

The Baptist Distinctives describe the local church's membership, leadership, practices, and relationships. Many have listed these distinctives in the form of an acrostic using the name Baptist.[66] This is an example:

*B*ible as the only rule of faith and practice

*A*utonomy of the local church

*P*riesthood of the believer

*T*wo Ordinances

*I*ndividual Soul Liberty

*S*eparation personal and ecclesiastical

*T*wo officers of the local church

The New Testament principles embraced by Baptists, and which are known as the distinctives of Baptist churches, include the observance of the ordinances. But, Baptist **beliefs about baptism and the Lord's Supper do not stand alone**. They are interconnected, being closely related to each other as well as to other cherished Baptist doctrines. Together, their practice provides for **the protection and propagation** of the principles of New Testament Christianity.

When we say, "our principles make us Baptists," we are not primarily speaking about the gospel. Many who would reject Baptist church principles would agree with the soteriology of most Baptists. Our distinctives reflect our body life. Baptist distinctives serve primarily to define the church and its ministry.

How do Baptists conduct worship? Because the Bible is the word

---

[66] I prefer to use the acrostic BRAPSIS, coined by Dr. Richard Weeks, Baptist historian and longtime professor at Maranatha Baptist Bible College. For the purpose of this chapter, I am using the more familiar acrostic.

of God, Baptist worship focuses on Bible teaching. The exposition of the Scriptures is foundational to New Testament Christianity.

How are we to be governed? Baptist believers are committed to obeying the teachings of the Bible. The Bible directs the local church to choose pastors to whom the members will be accountable and who will lead the church in observing all the commands of Christ.

How do we relate to one another? Baptists believe in the priesthood of every believer and practice congregational church government. The New Testament recognizes both individual and corporate responsibilities for believers.

How do we relate to human government? Baptists believe in being separate from the government. The church has no political authority, and the government or state has no authority in church affairs.

How do we relate to other churches? Each church is autonomous. They are self-governing, self-supporting, and self-propagating. No church or group of churches has authority over another.

How are members admitted? Baptists believe in a regenerated, immersed church membership (see chapter 8). This practice calls for scriptural baptism after conversion.

The Baptist distinctives overlap and are inter-related to each other, especially as they relate to the ordinances.

1. The Bible as the only rule of faith and practice

The message of the Christian faith is, therefore, rooted in and circumscribed by God's own revealed word and not in the authoritative words of men.

- "They that gladly received the word…" Acts 2:41
- "They continued steadfastly in the apostles' doctrine" Acts 2:42

Their faith was based upon an understanding of the word of God. They received the word that was preached by Peter and was based in the Old Testament Scriptures. It required mental maturity to believe and to obey God. Infants do not qualify. Personal faith was the prerequisite for baptism!

Baptists differ from other Protestant denominations in that they find their authority in the New Testament alone. This claim instantly sets Baptists apart from Reformed models that look to the Old Testament and Episcopal models that depend on tradition for their principal authority.[67]

Reformed denominations, following the church authority of Catholic tradition, look to the church councils to authenticate the canon of Scripture and to determine doctrinal orthodoxy. Greg Bahnsen rightly observes,

> ...the canon is not the product of the Christian church. The church has no authority to control, create, or define the Word of God. **Rather, the canon controls, creates and defines the church**... Authority is inherent in those writings from the outset, and the church simply confesses this to be the case (emphasis added).[68]

Similarly, the ordinances are not the product of the church, but they are the pictures commanded by God to be practiced in the church by all believers. These ordinances define the churches and are not devised by the churches. They point to the person and work of Christ for personal salvation, but they do not impart that salvation. The ordinances also lay the foundation for church polity.

2. Autonomy

- Be baptized (Acts 2:38)
- When ye come together in the church (1 Cor. 11:18)

---

[67] David Saxon, 'The Logic Of BRAPSIS,' Maranatha Baptist University, September 1, 2006.
[68] Greg Bahnsen, "The Concept and Importance of Canonicity," Reformed.org, Accessed January 10, 2024. https://reformed.org/bible/the-concept-and-importance-of-canonicity-by-greg-bahnsen/.

Both ordinances speak to autonomy at the most fundamental level. The local church determines the qualification of candidates for baptism and determines who may sit at the Lord's Table. Each Baptist church has the right of determination in such matters, but all decisions must be in harmony with Bible teaching.

The local church is the highest authority on earth in spiritual matters. There was no higher appeal given by Christ in dealing with personal issues between brethren (Matthew 18:18-20); no denomination or ecclesiastical appointee has the authority to dictate policy or make decisions for the local church.

3. Priesthood of the believer

Just as local churches cannot be made to answer to manmade institutions, believers need neither the church to give us authorized interpretations of Scripture, nor a priest to hear our confession or dispense grace to us. Believers are priests, saints and ministers of the New Covenant.

The priesthood of the believer is recognized in the ordinance of baptism as the newly converted one personally testifies that he has been born again through faith in Jesus Christ. Likewise, in observing the Lord's Supper, he examines himself in relationship to faithful obedience to Christ and His commands.

4. Individual soul liberty

Soul freedom relates to baptism and the Lord's Supper in that a person's participation in both are voluntary, never forced. In baptism, the person being baptized is not passive but active, both in calling for baptism, and in the reality that he must co-operate in the immersion. Warns says,

> The original Christian baptism demands the free personality of the baptized person. *No one can be a Christian, a follower of Christ by compulsion*. Membership in the church presupposes *the personal decision of the individual*. This personal element, the foundation of Biblical Christianity, is eliminated by infant

baptism (emphasis added).[69]

The recognition of soul liberty as fundamental to Biblical Christianity, is a repudiation of the state church model. Again, speaking against infant baptism and the state church that endorses it, Warns states,

> The act of believer's baptism is a renunciation of every National and State Church in general. Regenerate immersed church membership is a declaration of war on the state church model.[70]

A contemporary writer, Steve Lemke, concurs:

> The affirmation of believer's baptism is in all major Baptist confessions... (and) is central to our identity as Baptists. The notion of sprinkling of infants to wash away their original sin is repugnant to Baptists throughout our history. This is not a peripheral issue for Baptists. Baptists have literally given their lives for this belief....[71]

Religious liberty is a doctrine most associated with Baptists and the quest for it is a glorious theme in Baptist church history. Colonial Baptists like John Leland saw congregational government and soul liberty in the churches as the ideal or model to follow for national politics. *The concept of soul liberty was learned through the function of the local church. As such, Baptists viewed this liberty as a right given by God.* And, consequently, a great many Baptists paid the ultimate price for their convictions while defending the soul liberty of their persecutors.

5. Separation

Personal separation is inherent in baptism as one dies to the old life and is raised to the new. The Lord's Supper is celebrated frequently because constant vigilance is necessary to keep one's

---

[69] Warns, *Baptism*, 270.

[70] Ibid, 240.

[71] Steve Lemke, "What Is A Baptist? Nine Marks that Separate Baptists from Presbyterians" (*Journal for Baptist Theology & Ministry,* Fall 2008), 20.

heart fixed on Christ and on obedience to His will.

Not only is ecclesiastical separation the necessary corollary of belief in autonomous churches, it is also upheld through both ordinances. Baptism associates the converted to a particular local church. By determining who may sit at the table, the local church is upholding their own doctrinal position.

It is the old conflict and antagonism between the state church and the church of believers which is at stake in the baptism question. *A church of believers, in the New Testament sense, will also attest its separation from the world* by also introducing scriptural baptism and scriptural celebration of the Lord Supper.[72]

Warns goes on to quote A. C. Underwood who says,

> *Baptists are testifying against much more than an isolated and relatively unimportant custom (infant baptism)*; they are testifying against the whole complex of ideas of which it was a symbol, out of which grew the conception of the Church as primarily a great sacramental institution, administered by a body of officials vested with spiritual powers in which ordinary Christians could not share (emphasis added).[73]

Nine of the thirteen original American colonies had state churches which were supported by the taxes of the general population. Infant baptism was utilized by the state churches to unite a person to the church and ultimately to the control of the government. Infant baptism and state tax revenues were the mechanisms essential for the continuation of these churches.

For example, two laws were passed by the early colonists in the fear that their state churches would lose their standing if a free church were allowed in a free land. Therefore, in November 1644, the general court of Massachusetts enacted a statute protecting the state church by mandating infant baptism. The law stated that

---

[72] Warns, *Baptism*, 265.
[73] A. C. Underwood, *A History of the English Baptists* (London: The Baptist Union Publications, 1947), 271, quoted in Warns, *Baptism*, 239.

anyone who:

> shall ever either openly **condemn or oppose the baptizing of**
> **infants** or go about secretly to seduce others from the
> approbation or use thereof shall purposely depart the
> congregation and the administration of the ordinance or shall
> deny the ordinance of magistry or their lawful rights and
> authority to make war or to punish outward breaches of the
> first table (of the Mosaic Law) and shall appear to the court
> willfully ... to continue therein after due time and means of
> conviction every such person or persons shall be sentenced to
> banishment (emphasis added).[74]

In 1662, the Virginian government passed the following statute:

> Whereas may schismaticall persons out of their aversenesse to
> the orthodox established religion, (Church of England) or out of
> the new fangled conceits of theri owne heretiall inventions,
> **refuse to have their children baptised....** Be it therefore
> enacted by the authority aforesaid, that all persons that, in
> contempt of the divine sacrament of baptisme, shall refuse
> when they may carry their child to a lawfull minister in that
> county to have them baptised, **shall ve amerced two thousand**
> **pouds of tobacco; halfe to informer and halfe to the publique**
> (emphasis added).[75]

Baptists with their emphasis upon soul liberty and total religious
freedom strongly opposed the sacramental practice of the
ordinances. They were openly detested and persecuted for
challenging the state church.

6. Two officers

One expression of local church autonomy is its ability under God
to choose its own leadership. Clearly, pastors, bishops, and elders
are seen as the same office in Baptist confessions, which no doubt

---

[74] William Hening, *The Statutes at Large, Vol. 11* (Richmond, VA: Printed for the
editor by J&G Cochran, 1823), 165-166.
[75] Hening, *The Statutes at Large*, 165-166.

get their guidance from Acts 20:17, 28 (elders, overseers, feed or shepherd the flock) and 1 Peter 5:1-2 (elders, feed the flock, oversight). There is no priesthood in the local church other than the members themselves. Therefore, in Baptist churches, there are no clerics which give authority to the ordinances. Since all believers in Christ are priests (1 Pet. 2:5; Rev. 5:10), there is no need for a priestly class to administer either baptism or the Lord's Supper.

Though the Lord's Supper has a definite individual component, as does baptism, it is observed in a local church context. That those invited to share in the Lord's Table hold the same theological views as that local church would be consistent. Similarly, it would be unthinkable for a local church to extend baptism to a person of divergent theological views.

However, as inconsistent and illogical as may be, I have personally been asked to perform baptisms by people persuaded that immersion is the only mode of baptism but who also intended to return to their pedobaptist church. More frequently, some attempt to join in a memorial observance of the Lord's Supper with the intention of returning to their sacramental church the next Sunday. In both cases, these are practical denials and even repudiations of the overall teachings of the ordinances.

In summary, when practiced biblically, the ordinances support Baptist polity. This conclusion, it may be argued, is self-confirming or circular. However, it is better to discern that a New Testament understanding of the ordinances as practiced by the Apostles, as well as the early church, and taught in the Scriptures demands Baptist polity rather than any other ecclesiastical form of church government.

The Bible is central to Baptist worship rather than some form of sacramentalism. Baptists understand that the grace of God comes to those who believe the gospel. Because faith comes by hearing the word of God (Rom. 10:17), then the preaching of the word must be central to church life and worship.

Baptists, by admitting to membership only persons who have believed the gospel and are immersed following their conversion, are protecting both the local church's health and testimony. Only saved individuals are equipped to exercise spiritual gifts within the body and to fulfill the "one another" responsibilities to its members.

Baptist polity is established by the ordinances regarding church membership. The baptism of believers is an admission to the local church membership and to the observation of the Lord's Supper. In this way, the ordinances define the church and its members. The local church is neither a nebulous group of those who attend on Sunday nor an open group including those who were born to parents who are members. Baptist polity through the ordinances draws specific lines for church inclusion and participation.

7

The Relationship of the Ordinances to Each Other

We have discussed the ordinances together as they relate to Christ, the local church and the believer. Now, let's further consider the relationship of the ordinances in local church practice.

The ordinances share gospel meaning.

Truly Baptist practice sharpens our focus on the need for evangelizing the lost. The ordinances remind us of the gospel. Baptism is first a confession of conversion while the Lord's Supper requires examination of one's true spiritual standing. The first testifies of the new birth, the other the continuing work of sanctification.

There is an overlap in the meaning of the two ordinances. They both proclaim the Lord's death and resurrection. Baptism recognizes the believer's walk in newness of life with our resurrected Lord, while the Lord's Supper speaks to our present life of fellowship with Him as the living Lord. Both ordinances are based upon His substitutionary atonement.

In picture, baptism raises us to follow while the bread and cup enable us to continue through faith in the word and confession of sin. Baptism symbolizes being raised by the Spirit; but symbolically in the Supper, the Spirit enlightens the bread, and He convicts believers to take the cup.

Baptism

In baptism, the believer testifies, "I need a transformation. I need new life. I have come to the end of myself and will now turn to the Lord for power to live for Him." Warns explains,

> "whoever submitted to baptism not only thereby acknowledged his faith in the Lord, but that he desired to belong to Him, that henceforth he would no more live unto himself, but unto Him who for his sake had died and risen again (Rom 6:4; 8:13).[76]

It seems very clear that infant baptism fails at this very point. How can parents and "godparents" believe or vouch for their children? Parents must believe for themselves; and their children must exercise personal faith as well. Of which faith, infants are completely incapable.

The man sees himself torn out of his former world; his life takes another direction, with another goal. The old has passed away; all things are become new. ...there is now given through baptism the testimony that: with Christ I am dead, buried, risen.[77]

Lord's Supper

In the Lord's Supper, the believer is testifying along these lines, "I desire to continue in fellowship with God. I have confessed sin that would separate me from enjoyment of fellowship. I am living by faith. I need the Lord continually. I am depending on Him."

Eating symbolizes our faith in the Lord Jesus. Jesus said that His

---

[76] Warns, *Baptism*, 28.
[77] Ibid.

body was broken "for you" (1 Cor. 11:24). The sinner through the Holy Spirit's conviction senses His need and sees Christ as His remedy. But he will not be saved until he actually believes. What a person eats is certainly his. The Supper reinforces this truth.

Eating is responding to a felt need called hunger. A hungry man never gets rid of his hunger by talking about eating, but by actually eating. Like eating, a person must partake of Christ by faith in His death for their sins and in the new life which He imparts.

If I don't eat the food, it doesn't do anything for me. It is the same with spiritual food. It doesn't profit anyone to merely acknowledge Jesus Christ's deity and moral qualities, if they never eat. Knowing the truth and talking about the truth does not meet the need of one's soul any more than uneaten food on the table will satisfy the need of one's body.

Eating must be done personally. No one can eat for another. There's no such thing as eating by proxy. Personal appropriation is necessary for every individual. Each man eats for himself and not for anyone else. And so, in coming to Christ, you must come to Him for yourself. Faith is your own act and deed—no one can believe for you, nor can you believe for another.

Believing is not a passive activity. We must be active and perform the personal act of appropriating the Lord Jesus to be our soul's meat and drink. Charles Spurgeon summarizes this thought well, as follows:

> What do I see on that table? I see bread there. Then I gather this humbling lesson—that *I cannot even keep myself in spiritual food*. I am such a pauper, such an utter beggar, that *my own table cannot furnish me with what I want* and I must come to the Lord's table—and *I must receive, through Him, the spiritual nutriment which my soul requires.*
>
> What do I see in the cup? I see the wine which is the token of His shed blood. *What does that say to me but that I still need*

cleansing? Oh, how I rejoice in that blessed text in John's first epistle—"If we walk in the light, as he is in the light, we have fellowship with one another!" And then what follows? That we do not need to make any more confession of sin, because we are quite cleansed from it?

Nothing of the sort. "And the blood of Jesus Christ his Son, cleanseth us from all sin." We still need the cleansing fountain even when we are walking in the light, as God is in the light— and we need to come to it every day. And what a mercy it is that the emblem sets forth the constant provision of purifying blood whereby we may be continually cleansed! As we partake of this cup, we must do so humbly, for thus it becomes us to come to the table of our Lord (emphasis added).[78]

The ordinances are distinct in purpose.

Baptism signifies a walk of new life, of a new direction, and of a new family association. We are raised to walk in newness of life (Rom. 6:1-3). The Lord's Supper not only reminds the believer of his justification and initial sanctification, but it cries out for progressive sanctification and spiritual accountability in the body.

Baptism emphasizes conversion, while the Lord's Supper primarily emphasizes sanctification. Spurgeon summarizes:

The other ordinance is the Lord's Supper; and, as baptism sets forth, typifies, (mark you, nothing more than typifies,) and is the emblem of the new birth, so the Lord's Supper is the emblem of the spiritual feeding of that new life. Now, though a man is born only once, he eats a great many more times than once, and drinks a great many more times than once. Indeed,

---

[78] Charles Spurgeon, "The Right Observance of the Lord's Supper," Sermon No. 2638, delivered June 4, 1882, The Metropolitan Tabernacle, Newington (London). https://www.spurgeongems.org/sermon/chs2638.pdf.

to eat and to drink often, are necessary to the maintenance of our life.[79]

A better understanding of the ordinances would give us gospel clarity. There is no sharp separation between justification and sanctification. These are distinct, as are the two ordinances, but they cannot be separated. Baptism is the introduction to the path of discipleship. The Great Commission commands baptism but then involves teaching believers to observe to do all things Christ has commanded. Those converted at Pentecost continued steadfastly in the Apostle's doctrine. Any belief that lacks commitment, instills no new spiritual desires or produces no change in behavior, is as insufficient as it is ineffective.

Therefore, the justification pictured in baptism naturally and normally results in the progressive sanctification pictured in the Lord's Supper with final, complete sanctification or glorification as its end. Henry Colby, writing nearly 170 years ago, stated:

> Baptism signifies our death to sin and our rising again to newness of life, our fellowship with the death and resurrection of Jesus Christ. It speaks of a change from one spiritual condition to another. It symbolizes the New Birth. But the Lord's Supper signifies the continuance and maintenance of that new life—the constant dependence of the believer upon Christ for spiritual support and growth.[80]

The ordinances differ in frequency and have a prescribed theological order.

1. Frequency

Baptism: In baptism, as a picture of the new birth, one dies to the old life and is raised to the new. Since regeneration is a once-for-all-time spiritual experience, a believer should only be baptized

---

[79] Charles Spurgeon, "Fencing the Table," Sermon No. 2865, delivered January 2, 1876, biblebb.com/files/spurgeon/2865.htm.
[80] Colby, *Restriction of the Lord's Supper*, 27–29.

once after conversion. However, it is common practice for believers to be rebaptized by a favorite preacher or in a "holy place." I have observed believers of many years being rebaptized in the Jordan River. The value of one's baptism is neither validated nor enhanced in these cases. It's not the esteem of the administrator or the place of the water, but the faith of the candidate that gives value to the ordinance of baptism.

Therefore, believer's baptism should not be repeated upon a believer's transfer from one local church to another. Rebaptism violates the picture of a once-for-all-time salvation.

However, this discussion does not include anyone who was sprinkled or poured, even after conversion. The New Testament mode of baptism is immersion and should be required of all believers. Immersion is the only valid form of baptism.

Lord's Supper: When the church met together on the first day of the week, they would have a fellowship meal, communion, and a sermon. The Love Feast, it seems, gradually faded away since it was a practice more of the time and culture, and not something specifically instituted by our Lord or the Apostles.

The Bible doesn't specify the frequency of observing the Lord's Supper but it must not be neglected. In the Supper we have a wonderful privilege of commemorating the death and anticipating the return of Christ.

The Lord's Supper is celebrated *often* because we need daily dependence and forgiveness. We must live by faith and dependence on Christ; and we must regularly confess sin to maintain our fellowship with the One who is faithful and just to forgive our sin. Constant spiritual vigilance is necessary to keep one's heart in fellowship with Christ and in obedience to His will. The Lord's Supper pictures this on-going process of sanctification.

Henry Colby's comment here is insightful:

> Baptism represents regeneration, a single event. The Lord's Supper represents our abiding trust, and ever recurring duty

and refreshment. Writers of various denominations have spoken of *baptism as the ordinance of initiation*, and of *the Lord's Supper as the ordinance of nutrition*. In this difference of meaning they have found one reason why a person is *baptized but once*, but partakes of *the Lord's Supper repeatedly* (emphasis added).[81]

The early church celebrated the Lord's Table daily (Acts 2:46) and it soon became a weekly pattern (Acts 20:7). Surely, in recent days, there has been a reaction against Catholicism's Mass and the Church of Christ who celebrate weekly. However, some fundamental churches in other countries observe the Supper weekly.

Johann Gerhard Oncken was the friend of the great English Baptist pastor, Charles Haddon Spurgeon. Spurgeon preached for the dedication of Oncken's new chapel in Hamburg, Germany sometime before 1884 when Oncken died. After describing the new building in some detail, along with Spurgeon's voice filling the place with a call to take of the water of life freely, we learn:

> The day closed in a very fitting manner, the ordinance of the Lord's Supper being observed. *Throughout the Baptist churches of Germany it was the custom to observe Communion weekly, and to that practice Spurgeon himself held dearly.* Oncken and Spurgeon were truly at one on all points of doctrine and practice besides being at one in their experience of persecution and hardship, and at one in their desire to train men 'to teach others also' (emphasis added).[82]

Spurgeon's view on the frequency of observing the Supper is clearly presented in his church. He emphatically preached:

---

[81] Colby, *Restriction of the Lord's Supper*, 27–29.
[82] Eric Hayden, "Johann Gerhard Oncken: Friend of Spurgeon," Banneroftruth.org, September 22, 2017, https://Banneroftruth.org/us /resources/articles/2017/johann-gerhard-oncken-friend-spurgeon/.

> *Shame on the Christian church that she put it off to once a month* and mar the first day of the week by depriving it of its glory in the meeting together for fellowship and breaking of bread and showing forth the death of Christ till he comes. They who once know *the sweetness of each Lord's day celebrating his supper*, will not be content, I am sure, to put it off to less frequent seasons. Beloved, when the Holy Ghost is with us, ordinances are wells to the Christian, wells of rich comfort and of near communion (emphasis added).[83]

Many Baptist churches have settled on a monthly observance to neither neglect nor become overly familiar with its observance. The Scripture says, "as often as" and not "as seldom as." Is a quarterly or yearly practice to be considered as "as often as" (1 Cor. 11:26)? Each local church should set the time and frequency. Clearly, the celebration of the Supper is not confined to Sunday morning worship. The Passover observance was at night and the Apostle Paul observed the Lord's Supper at night in conjunction with his preaching in Troas (Acts 20:7).

2. Order

There is a chronological order in the ordinances which churches ought to strictly observe. Believer's immersion precedes communion, or the Lord's Table. Believer's immersion, picturing the death, burial, and resurrection of our Lord Jesus Christ, speaks of our **union** with Christ while the Lord's table speaks of our **communion** with Him. Union always precedes communion!

The order of the ordinances has clear theological significance. Baptism comes before the Lord's Supper just as justification comes before sanctification. You must begin with Christ before you can continue with Him. Baptism is about conversion; the Lord's Supper is about fellowship.

---

[83] Charles Spurgeon, "Songs of Deliverance," Sermon No. 763, Delivered July 28, 1867, Metropolitan Tabernacle Pulpit, Newington (London), https://www.spurgeongems.org/sermon/chs763.pdf.

These ordinances speak to body life as well. Baptism is entrance into the local church whereas the Lord's Supper relates to fellowship with God's people in the local church. Both ordinances were commanded by Christ to be observed in the churches by the members of the church. All obedient disciples of Jesus Christ must be baptized and all baptized disciples are to be church members who participate in the Lord's Supper.

Acts 2 describes the order of the ordinances. This description becomes a prescription as we observe in Acts the practice of the early church and as we study the epistles which give the theological framework.

The order of the ordinances protects both the gospel and New Testament church purity. They teach us about Christ, His person and work, but they also direct us in our responsibilities as local churches. The order of the ordinances is most important to local church ecclesiology, just as regenerate and immersed church membership is to being Baptist.

It is in relation to this conviction that Baptists are often denigrated as bigoted and extreme. But understanding that baptism is a prerequisite to participation in the Lord's Supper is a very important theological point. Baptists realize that the ordinances have a chronological order. Believer's immersion always precedes the Lord's Table. Furthermore, the ordinances have been given to local churches. As a result of these principles, Baptists have been unwilling to participate with unbaptized believers at the Lord's Table, opening themselves up to the charge of being uncharitable and extreme. But, Baptists are simply attempting to be faithful to the word of God and the testimony of the gospel.

The order of the ordinances is derived theologically and not from one specific text of Scripture. Consider the words from a Baptist leader writing in 1880:

> We do not profess to be able to accomplish the task proposed
> by producing any single passage of Scripture, declaring directly

and unequivocally: "Thou shalt not come to the Lord's Table before baptism." But we do claim that it may be proved by a strictly logical argument, based upon the teachings of Scripture, that baptism is a prerequisite.[84]

Henry Colby succinctly summarizes,

...baptism should be first, and the Lord's Supper second.... Now, if Christ established two ordinances to represent these two truths, is it not evident that the observance of the Lord's Supper implies that baptism has preceded, and that **to put the Lord's Supper before baptism is to destroy the consistency of their symbolism**? If, in spiritual as well as in physical life, **birth precedes sustenance by food**, and if there are two corresponding ordinances, one of which is observed only once, and the other from time to time, do we need anything further to show what Christ's intention was as to their order?
..."**baptism** is the act by which the new-born believer outwardly and symbolically puts off his body of sin and puts on Christ, and thus solemnly enrolls himself among the followers of the Redeemer." Its place is, therefore, at **the threshold of the confessed Christian life. But the Lord's Supper is the ordinance in which Christ's disciples revive from time to time**, by means of touching material emblems, their memory of the love he showed by suffering for them, and their expectation of his coming in glory (emphasis added).[85]

Alex Hay makes a clear case for the order of ordinances by drawing attention to baptism's purpose of giving a conversion testimony. He writes,

Baptism is merely the believer's public testimony, exceedingly important as such but nothing more. It is right that a convert should not be received at the Lord's table before baptism, not because baptism confers necessary grace, but simply **because there can hardly be certainty regarding the genuineness of**

---

[84] Gear, *The Relation of Baptism*, 21.
[85] Colby, *Restriction of the Lord's Supper*, 27–29.

the conversion of one who is not willing to take the first step of obedience and make public confession of his faith. For baptism the early church did not demand spiritual maturity but only clear evidence of conversion (emphasis added).[86]

To sit at the table before baptism is like one enjoying or sharing church life before joining. It is picturing Christian growth and maturity without conversion and church association. Should one seek to grow independently of church commitment? Does the Bible teach that one may be obedient to Christ without identification with His church? The answer to both questions is no.

The inspired word on the matter was delivered by the Lord to Paul and then to the church at Corinth. The Lord's Supper is observed when believing members come together (1 Cor. 11:18,20,33) in the church. Their unity is described by calling the members "one bread" (1 Cor. 10:17) and they are to tarry one for another (1 Cor 11:33).

That this order of the ordinances was invariably observed in apostolic times is, indeed, generally admitted.[87] Acts 2 begins with the clear preaching of the gospel message and the reception of the same word or message. Baptism, church addition, and the continuing in the word is followed in that order. The Lord's Supper was celebrated as part of this continuance.

As clearly as the ordinances have individual symbolic meaning, it is certain that their order is symbolic as well. Writing in 1853, Henry Colby states:

If the things symbolized have no *necessary* order, then, of course, the order of the ordinances which symbolize them would not be significant. But if the things symbolized stand to each other in a necessary relation, as first and second; and if

---

[86] Alex Rattray Hay, *The New Testament Order for Church and Missionary* (Eugene, OR: Wipf and Stock Publishers, 2010), 310–313.
[87] Colby, *Restriction of the Lord's Supper*, 25.

that relation is positively declared and strenuously enforced in the New Testament, as a truth to be proclaimed and defended, — then we are compelled to believe that the Lord, who established the symbols in this order, and meant each to have a meaning separately, also meant them to have a meaning in their sequence. In other words, he meant *their very order* to be symbolical.[88] (Emphasis his)

Baptism is before church membership and the Lord's Supper is for members.

Gear speaks of church membership as the 'intermediate' relationship which exists between the ordinances and which establishes their necessary order. He writes:

There is a divinely established relation between the ordinances of baptism and the Lord's Supper, growing out of their nature and design, and necessitated by their mutual relation to … church membership. …Much has been said about the relation of baptism to the Lord's Supper, with a tacit assumption that its relation is direct and immediate, ignoring the *intermediate term of church membership*. But this term should never be ignored, for it is through and on account of it that the relation exists between the two ordinances. The argument may be stated thus: Baptism was designed and established as an initial rite, preceding and prerequisite to church membership. The Lord's Supper was designed and established as a church ordinance, following church membership, and constituting one of the privileges of church fellowship. It follows that baptism must precede the Lord's Supper. Or it may be stated more briefly and syllogistically thus: *Baptism is prerequisite to church membership; church membership is prerequisite to the Lord's Supper; therefore, baptism is prerequisite to the Lord's Supper.* Nothing can be clearer than that, if the premises of this argument are true, the

---

[88] Colby, *Restriction of the Lord's Supper*, 30.

conclusion is logical and irresistible.[89] (Bold italic emphasis mine, italic emphasis his)

Gear continues by calling baptism "an initial rite," a "first duty," and an "initiatory badge of discipleship":

> *Baptism is prerequisite to church membership.* This proposition hardly needs proof, for it is universally held as true, by Pedobaptists as well as by Baptists. Methodists, Episcopalians, Presbyterians, Lutherans, Congregationalists, Baptists, Free-will Baptists, Roman Catholics, and other bodies, of whatsoever denomination, ...are all agreed in holding that baptism must precede admission to church membership; and all alike require some act which they consider baptism, as a necessary condition and prerequisite of church fellowship. The common consent of Christendom to this position has its abundant warrant in the word of God. The ordinance was designed and instituted as an initial rite. It is the first duty required of believers after repentance and faith, and is Christ's own appointed mode of professing allegiance to him before the world. It is in its nature an initiatory badge of discipleship, required to be administered and received before admission to the church.[90] (Emphasis his)

Henry Colby agrees and relates the practice in the early church as follows:

> We find that such was the practice of the churches in the days succeeding the apostles. Neander refers to the Supper, during the first three centuries, when he says: "At this celebration, as may be easily concluded, no one could be present who was not a member of the Christian church, and incorporated into it by the rite of baptism." In speaking of the faithful and catechumens, in the first century, Mosheim says: "The former were such as had been solemnly admitted into the church by baptism, and who might be present at all the parts of religious

---

[89]Gear, *Relation of Baptism*, 21–23.
[90] Ibid, 23–24.

worship. ***The latter, not yet having received baptism, were not admitted to the sacred Supper*** (emphasis added)."[91]

What about children? Should a child partake of the Lord's Supper before they are baptized? Some have said, "My son doesn't understand baptism." Well, if they don't understand baptism, they won't understand the Lord's Supper, and may not understand salvation! Admission to the Lord's Supper is predicated upon church membership, and church membership requires baptism. Children who have truly believed on the Lord Jesus are held to the same scriptural requirements as adult believers when it comes to church membership and the observing of the ordinances.

Should we admit pedobaptists to the Supper? This is a reoccurring question that comes from many due to a perceived need for Christian graciousness or hospitality. So perhaps this question may appear redundant considering the previous extended arguments. However, errors abound and the tendency for most leaders is to become more tolerant and welcoming.

The heartfelt desire of those who have received grace is to extend grace, by receiving to the Table all who profess faith in Christ, and who have received a form of "baptism" by sprinkling, whether before or after their conversion. In truth, infant baptism by any means is not biblical baptism. As we have seen, the Bible teaches that regeneration must proceed immersion. Believer's immersion, and not sprinkling or pouring, is the only valid baptism. Gear affirms the same:

> Now, in the face of these Scriptures, if it be true, as we believe it is, that infant baptism and the substitution of sprinkling and pouring for baptism are ***heretical departures*** from the teachings of the New Testament, from the ordinances as they were delivered to the saints, ***we are left no discretion: we are bound to exclude those who practice them from our church***

---

[91] Colby, *Restriction of the Lord's Supper*, 35.

> *fellowship*. But it was especially designed to show, in this connection, that the Lord's Supper is a peculiar privilege of the church membership.
>
> This is unquestionably proven by the grant of excommunicating power to the church. We have thus established the second premise of our argument. The argument then stands, as a whole, impregnable; and the conclusion follows irresistibly: Therefore, baptism is prerequisite to the Lord's Supper (emphasis added).[92]

It is rightly argued that the order of the ordinances is necessary to complete the picture of the salvation of a believer. The ordinances were meant to be practiced together in order to give comprehensive understanding of the fruit of the gospel in the believer. Though Colby confuses the Kingdom and the church, his basic argument is true. Regeneration is a prerequisite to participation in church life and to true worship. He states:

> Thus the significance of the order is necessary to give completeness to the ritual expression. Surely, Baptists, more than all others, may be expected to maintain it strictly. For this prerequisiteness of regeneration to all participation in God's kingdom is the very truth, which, in our judgment, has been obscured by the errors of Pedobaptism. If it had received its due prominence, there would have been no practice of infant sprinkling, as a substitute for the immersion of the believer...; no recognition of unconverted persons as members of a church of Christ; and no union of "Church and State." Against these evils, **Baptists** have ever felt called to protest. They **have not been contending for the mere forms of the ordinances; but for the true meaning of those ordinances**, as set forth in the only adequate forms—the forms which Christ has appointed.... Every real Baptist church and minister proclaim and defend these truths still. **We should see to it, therefore, that our gospel in symbol runs parallel to our gospel in words,** that

---

[92] Gear, *Relation of Baptism*, 30-33.

neither is robbed of its completeness; but as we ever follow our statements concerning the new birth and the believer's privileges, by *declaring that the former is prerequisite to the latter, so let the ordinance which signifies the former always be put before that which signifies the latter. Let us not, by reversing their sequence, curtail their language at the very point where, in our verbal proclamations of truth, we make the strongest stand* (emphasis added).[93]

Why can't Baptist churches allow the individual to follow his own conscience?

Because it is called the "Lord's Supper," using the possessive, it is sometimes assumed that it is not the Table of any particular church. However, the local church is the custodian of the Lord's Table; it is to be preserved and practiced as the Lord has directed. The Lord's Supper is a local church ordinance to be observed according to biblical commands and principles. The Baptist distinctive of soul liberty doesn't give any pedobaptist the right to demand others, in this case the local Baptist church, to endorse their fallacious understanding of Scripture by allowing them to participate in the Lord's Supper. This is the historical and biblical position of Baptists. Colby writes:

The Table is indeed the Lord's, in the sense that it is his gift to his church. But as the visible church is to spread it and maintain it, so *she is to guard it and all the truth concerning it with the same fidelity with which she is to guard all the other truths of his word.* This responsibility he has laid upon her, and she cannot put it off. It is because it is the Lord's Table and not one of her own invention, that she cannot, in the fulfilment of her solemn charge, welcome to it any but those whom she is convinced he regards as qualified. *In the same sense in which the Table is the Lord's Table, baptism is the Lord's baptism*; that is, it is an ordinance which he has established, and to the observance of which he has attached a blessing. But *we would*

---

[93] Colby, *Restriction of the Lord's Supper*, 31-32.

not receive a man for baptism merely because he was sincere in believing himself to be a fit candidate. We first examine and pronounce upon his fitness (emphasis added).[94]

Colby strengthens the argument by taking the inclusion of pedobaptists to its logical end. Opening the Communion Table to those not Scripturally baptized would lead to the opening of membership to the same individuals. It would be inconsistent to do otherwise. Consider his logic as follows:

In like manner the church is to decide as to the qualifications of those who come to the Supper. She is to guard both ordinances with equal fidelity. Indeed, we might say, that as the Table is the Lord's Table, so the church is the Lord's church. If Pedobaptists are to be welcomed to the former, on the ground of their sincerity in thinking that they have been baptized, then consistency would require that for the same reason they should be received into the latter. *Inviting the unbaptized to the Lord's Supper leads logically to inviting them to church membership*; and we need not go far to find instances in which persons, having adopted the former, have found themselves constrained to adopt the latter also. If a Baptist church should thus adopt the principle of welcoming the unbaptized to church membership, then what would prevent it, as soon as the majority of the members were Pedobaptists, from ceasing to be a Baptist church? (emphasis added).[95]

Perhaps this slippery slope would not result in the worst fall or the most extreme consequences in every case. Yet, when the ordinances are under attack, the gospel itself is in danger. The ordinances support and promote the gospel as well as protect the integrity of the church membership. When these safeguards are removed, the local church is more likely to admit the unregenerate into membership. Colby continues:

She would be renouncing her mission, casting into the dust the

---

[94] Colby, *Restriction of the Lord's Supper*, 41-42.
[95] Ibid.

crown which Christ placed upon her head, and *leaving her own purity unprotected*. She would be assuming a position which would shut her mouth even against the popular fallacy, that "it is no matter what a man believes as long as he is sincere"—a fallacy that is destroying many souls. She must not do this. *She must not do anything which would lead her to be unfaithful to her guardianship of the truth*. Without claiming infallibility of judgment, she is yet bound to withhold her fellowship from everything which she believes to be contrary to God's word (emphasis added).[96]

The refusal to receive Pedobaptists, or anyone who has not been scripturally immersed, to the Lord's Table, is not a statement of spiritual superiority. This is not saying that all pedobaptists lack Christian character or are not Christians at all. Baptists do not declare superiority in Christian virtues or infer that they are better Christians in every regard than those who practice infant baptism. What we do assert is that we are convinced the command of our Lord to baptize means immersion, and that it may only be administered to believers. Infant sprinkling fails on both points.

It is likely that many pedobaptists are sincere in their beliefs, but they are wrong nonetheless. They may be truly converted and living in obedience to the Lord in other matters, but disobedient and accountable to the Lord. Again Colby offers insight saying,

So far are we from denying that members of Pedobaptist churches are good Christians, that we love and honor them as brethren, servants of the same Master with ourselves. We do not say that they are not just as good Christians as we are. Nay, our position concerning the Lord's Supper does not declare that they may not be, on the whole, better Christians than we are—more humble, more devoted, more zealous. It does not interfere with the real recognition by us, of any of their virtues. *It simply declares, so far as it has a bearing toward them, that they have omitted that which we are solemnly convinced is*

---

[96] Colby, *Restriction of the Lord's Supper*, 44.

one requirement of our Lord, and which they ought to fulfil before they sit down to the Lord's Table (emphasis added).[97]

The ordinances are perpetual.

These are perpetual ordinances to be practiced until Jesus comes again; no one has the right to change them or discontinue their practice. Matthew 28:18-20 says that the Lord is personally present in the church ministry of evangelizing, baptizing and teaching. Because He promises the blessing of His presence as we fulfill the Great Commission throughout the Church Age, water baptism is commanded by Christ until the end of the age. It is clear that this command was given to others beside the eleven Apostles because it was to be carried out for centuries after the natural lives of the Apostles. Evangelism, baptism, and teaching together are to continue until the end of the age.

The Great Commission was practiced by the Apostle Paul. He carried the gospel to many cities, baptizing or supervising the baptism of many converts. It is said that Paul only baptized a few disciples (1 Cor. 1:14-17). This may be true, but he taught and approved baptism just as Jesus did.

Since the church continues until Christ comes in the event called the Rapture, new believers will be saved and baptized until He comes. Baptism will continue until the end of the age.

Since there will always be living believers in the churches until Jesus comes, there will always be those who are being progressively sanctified. The Lord's Supper will be practiced in all churches until all church-age believers are glorified at the Rapture.

> *(1 Corinthians 11:26) For as often as ye eat this bread, and drink this cup, ye do shew the Lord's death till he come.*

---

[97] Colby, *Restriction of the Lord's Supper*, 5-6.

8

Regenerate, Immersed Church Membership

The New Testament requires, and therefore Baptists have long held, that the local church must be comprised of a regenerated and immersed church membership. Acts 2:41 provides the pattern traced throughout the Book of Acts: they first **believed**, then were **baptized**, and only then **belonged**. As one follows the advance of the gospel recorded in the Book of Acts, it is evident that this *description* of the first local church becomes a *prescription* for all churches. This single truth may be the most important identifier of a New Testament Baptist Church.

In this one verse, Scripture rules out infant baptism, because personal faith was necessary, while simultaneously excluding from membership those who are not baptized. Further, it teaches persons must be able to believe and to choose to be baptized, before they become, at baptism, immediately associated with a local body of believers.

Regenerate, Immersed Church Membership Guards the Gospel

Contrary to those churches who trace their roots to the Reformation, the most important point that Baptists derive from the Scriptures regarding the local church, is the makeup of its membership. Consider how the following Reformed denominations confuse the gospel in baptizing and admitting infants into their assemblies:

The Westminster Confession of Faith of 1646 teaches that baptism admits recipients into the visible Church, engrafts them into Christ, causes regeneration, and results in remission of sins.[98] It also states, "the efficacy of baptism is not tied to that moment of time wherein it is administered; grace promised is not only offered, but...conferred by the Holy Ghost, to such (whether of age or infants)...."[99]

Presbyterian: "Being washed with the water of baptism, we receive new life in Christ. In the words of the PC (USA) Directory for Worship: 'The baptism of children witnesses to the truth that God's love claims us before we are able to respond in faith....'"[100]

Christian Reformed Church: Because "infants as well as adults are in God's covenant and are his people," they, "no less than adults, are promised the forgiveness of sin" and thus "by baptism... should be received into the Christian church."[101]

Wisconsin Lutheran: In the Scripture, "baptism is *not a mere symbol ... not just a ceremony* done to connect someone outwardly to a church. *God is at work through baptism. He is connecting us to Christ's death and resurrection.* All of his mercy

---

[98] *Westminster Confession of Faith 1646, XXVIII.I.*
[99] Ibid, *XXVIII.VI.*
[100] Paul Galbreath, "Sacraments," 34.
[101]Zacharius Ursinus, et al, *Heidelberg Catechism*, trans. Reformed Church, 1978 (Heidelberg, Germany: University of Heidelberg, 1563), Q. and A. 74, https://heidelblog.net/catechism.

and grace are directed at the person being baptized. *The Holy Spirit is giving the new life of faith in Jesus*" (emphasis added).[102]

In summary, the Reformed confessions consistently teach a conjunction between baptism and regeneration:

> The confessions teach that baptism is an external sign of an inward reality (regeneration and cleansing from sin) and *that baptism actually confers the inward reality which it signifies.* The power of baptism, however, resides in the Holy Spirit rather than the act of baptism itself. Further, *the application of the grace conferred in baptism* is not tied to the time at which it is administered. The promise offered in baptism is conditional on faith and repentance, which may occur at a time later than the act of baptism (emphasis added).[103]

In Acts 2, the subjects of baptism were already *identifiable converts* who were professing their personal faith by public immersion. Those who are being saved (v.47) are *the only proper candidates for membership*, and these are spoken of as "*believers*" (v.44). Steve Lemke writes,

> The affirmation of believer's baptism is in all major Baptist confessions... [and] is central to our identity. The notion of sprinkling of infants to wash away their original sin is repugnant to Baptists throughout our history. This is not a peripheral issue; Baptists have literally given their lives for this belief....[104]

Dr. William Pettingill, co-author of the Scofield Bible, wrote: "... *Infant baptism is responsible for sending more people to hell than any other cause.*" He continued:

> ... How did it come about? It resulted from the doctrine of

---

[102]Joel D. Otto, "Alive in Christ: An Exegetical Study of Colossians 2:6–15," (Wisconsin Lutheran Seminary Essay File, 2010). http://essays.wisluthsem.org:8080/handle/123456789/3545

[103]Robert W. A. Letham, *The Westminster Assembly: Reading Its Theology in Historical Context* (Phillipsburg, NJ: P&R Publishing, 2009), 338–339.

[104]Lemke, "What Is A Baptist," 20.

baptismal regeneration, the teaching that water baptism is essential to salvation. It was natural for those holding this teaching to believe that everybody should be baptized as soon as possible, and so baptism of unconscious infants came into vogue among many of the churches. *These two grievous errors, baptismal regeneration and infant baptism . . . have caused more bloodshed and persecution than all other errors combined*. It is reliably estimated that over fifty million Christians were put to death during the 'dark ages' . . . mainly because they rejected these two errors and insisted that salvation was the gift of God, apart from works or ceremonies (emphasis added).[105]

The importance of the baptism of believers must not be minimized; it reminds the church of the clear gospel. In contrast, the sprinkling of infants miscommunicates the gospel in at least two ways: 1) It focuses on the church as the means to salvation and 2) it fails to emphasize personal repentance and faith in the death, burial, and resurrection of Jesus.

Regenerate, Immersed Church Membership Protects the Church

The New Testament Epistles were written to believers and to churches comprised of believers. These letters, in giving the theological framework for church organization and practice, make apparent that regenerate, immersed church membership provides for *the protection and propagation* of both the church and the gospel.

Sadly, many churches today, and especially Reformed churches, are made up largely of unsaved individuals who are admitted through infant baptism. This cannot be the pattern for a church that is devoted to holiness and righteousness in all areas of life as

---

[105] William Leroy Pettingill, *The Evils of Infant Baptism* (St. Paul, MN: Northland Publishing Co., 1947), 104-105.

well as the faithful preaching of the gospel.

As Baptists, we believe that the local church is obligated to reflect as accurately as humanly possible the body of Jesus Christ. This practice is strikingly opposed to most of professing Christianity, and particularly those who hold to some form of Reformed or Covenant Theology.

As Baptist dispensationalists we:

- Employ a normal-literal interpretation of Scripture.
- Recognize a difference between Israel and the church.
- Believe that the Scripture teaches, and that God has promised a literal, future Millennial Kingdom for Israel.

Reformed theologians interpret various Bible passages allegorically. They see only one people of God, finding the promises to Israel fulfilled in the church. With this methodology, they believe the future Millennial Kingdom promises to Israel are fulfilled in an allegorical way in the church.

But, when one rightly divides the word of truth, national Israel is seen as having an important future in the plan of God. We believe that a normal interpretation of Scripture reveals that there are dozens of prophecies yet to be fulfilled. We see the promises for Israel as distinct from the church and that many of these prophecies can only find their fulfillment in a literal, 1000-year earthly reign of Messiah Jesus, in Jerusalem, upon a literal throne of David, in a physical temple, as the throne room of His Millennial authority and worship.

> *(Romans 11:25-26) For I would not, brethren, that ye should be ignorant of this mystery, lest ye should be wise in your own conceits; that blindness in part is happened to Israel, **until** the fulness of the Gentiles be come in. And so all Israel **shall be saved.***

If the church is to be made up only of believers, then Baptist churches are correct in their practice to accept into their membership only those who have professed both by word and by scriptural baptism that they belong to Christ. No allegorical interpretation that equates Israel with the Church, or circumcision with baptism, is permitted. God has two distinct purposes and two distinct people in regard to Israel and the Church.

The importance of believer's baptism must not be minimized; it is the proper safeguard to a regenerate church membership. Do we really believe in believer's baptism by immersion? Are we really committed to a regenerate church? Each church will have to answer these questions as they advance the gospel and build the church.

Baptist commitment to the baptism of believers by immersion is historically recognized as essential to membership in a Baptist church. Bill Pinson, Director of the Texas Baptist Heritage Center and Executive Director Emeritus of the Baptist General Convention of Texas, said,

> A variety of reasons may cause some modern Baptists to downplay believer's baptism by immersion. Possibilities include the influence of "ecumenical evangelism" that stresses commonly held beliefs over denominational differences; the influence of Calvinism in some Baptist circles; a desire to be non-judgmental and tolerant; a postmodern worldview that questions exclusive claims of truth or "right" methods; and a lack of understanding about distinctive Baptist beliefs.

> For some churches, the baptism issue may be reduced to a question of marketing. The requirement of baptism by immersion as an act of the believer's public profession raises the social "cost" of church membership, leading some churches to compromise a commitment to believer's baptism as a prerequisite for membership.[106]

---

[106] ABP News, "Baptism meanings and methods spark debate among some Baptists" (Dallas: Baptist News Global, June 22, 2006), https://baptistnews.com /article/baptism-meanings-and-methods-spark-debate-among-some-baptists/#.XQkMdYhKhPY.

Mormons and Jews who convert to Christ are often rejected by their families when they are baptized. This rejection is also common for those who are baptized on some mission fields outside of the USA. There has always been a great social cost to following Jesus Christ. Obeying the word of God has often been in contradiction to the practices of established religion.

Why would anyone choose to be a Baptist? Historically, Baptists have been a persecuted people. They have been persecuted by both Rome and the Reformers. They were forced to worship in caves, catacombs and the cold forests of the Soviet Empire. In the colonial days of this nation, Baptists of Virginia were imprisoned for preaching the gospel without a state license.

Only later in America, with the constitutional guarantee of religious liberty, have we observed Baptists receiving the privileges available to others. Baptists have risen to the highest levels of society, but generally have been composed of the lower classes.

Regenerate, Immersed Church Membership Protects the Authority of the Scriptures

Baptists differ from Reformed denominations in that they find their authority for all church matters, not in tradition, but in the Scriptures alone – especially the New Testament.

Adoniram Judson was the first Baptist missionary sent from the U.S., but when he sailed from our shores he was a Congregationalist. In anticipation of meeting the Baptist missionary William Carey in India, he was compelled to study infant baptism and personally settle the subject from the Bible once and for all. A letter by Mr. Judson stated his conclusion: "the immersion of a professing believer is the only Christian baptism."[107] The couple was baptized on Sept. 6, 1812 in Calcutta. Ann wrote, "thus we are confirmed Baptists, not because we

---

[107] David Cummins, *This Day in Baptist History III* (David L. Cummins, 2006), 499.

wanted to be, but because the truth compelled us to be."[108]

The authoritative Scriptures consistently demonstrate that baptism is for those capable of intelligent faith in Jesus Christ. Even the account of the Philippian Jailor, which has been twisted by many, clearly demonstrates the baptism of believers. Paul and Silas spoke the word of the Lord to the jailor and his entire household. The household is then baptized. The Philippian jailor is found rejoicing and "believing in God with all his house." The whole household hears the Word, believes, and is baptized (Acts 16:32-34)!

We read in Acts 2:41 that those who "gladly received the word were baptized." Their faith was based on an understanding of the Word of God; the New Testament church received the Word preached by Peter based in the Old Testament Scriptures. It required some measure of mental maturity to believe and to obey the command to be baptized (Acts 2:38). Infants do not qualify. Personal faith was, and remains today, the Biblical prerequisite for baptism!

Regenerate, Immersed Church Membership Protects True Fellowship

The early church was comprised of believers unified around apostolic teaching. This doctrine became the ground of true fellowship or partnership in ministry (Acts 2:42). It is impossible for those who are unconverted to truly partner in spiritual work. The addition of unsaved individuals to the local church is not at all neutral. Having their participation in local church ministry will have tragic consequences. It will become a hindrance to the fulfillment of the Great Commission in both the evangelism of the lost and the edification of the local church. The unconverted cannot be expected to desire or model personal evangelism, become effective teachers of truth, or to have the mind of Christ

---

[108] David Cummins, *This Day in Baptist History: 366 Daily Devotions Drawn from the Baptist Heritage* (Greenville, SC: Bob Jones University Press, 1993), 69.

in decisions.

Regenerate, Immersed Church Membership Protects the Mission of the Church

Notice that the *saved* were added daily to the church (Acts 2:47). The apostles sought to win converts and those converts comprised the church. The salvation of souls produced church members (41). This is how Christ builds His church today. Without this focus, the local church is easily distracted into false missions like kingdom building, dominion theology, or the political state church.

Regenerate, Immersed Church Membership Promotes Evangelism

The early church modeled baptism and church association as fruits of conversion, not the cause of conversion. The Baptist practice of regenerate, immersed church membership sharpens our focus on the need for evangelizing the lost. As a corollary, any method of evangelism that does not result in the increase of church members ought to be examined as to its authenticity.

Crisis Conversion

Baptists believe in crisis, point-in-time conversion, or being born again. Passing from death to life occurs instantly upon faith (John 5:24) and is not a process. Covenant theology generally calls for a prolonged instructional process, catechism, and confirmation; Baptists characteristically work and pray for a point-in-time conversion of our children.

Since Reformed churches characteristically associate regeneration with baptism, personal faith can come years after regeneration, and in the case of infants, always does. Consequently, members of Reformed churches seldom speak of being saved at a point in time and are likely to view their children as "safe" because they were baptized as infants and included in the covenant.

Baptists recognize that even those closest to us, our own

139

offspring, need to be converted. Baptists seek to win all individuals to Christ—especially the lost young ones within the homes of our congregation and in our Sunday schools—knowing that none are saved by church ritual or association.

In response to Peter's preaching on Pentecost, there was a conscious, individual decision to receive the Word, which is to believe in Jesus (Acts 2:41,44). To receive the Word was to receive the teaching of Peter concerning Jesus being both Lord and Messiah (Acts 2:36), crucified according to the plan of God (Acts 2:23), raised from the dead (Acts 2:24, 32) and seated at the right hand of God (Acts 2:25).

Those who had a credible testimony of conversion were candidates for baptism. They were *identifiable converts* who had a personal assurance of salvation professing their faith in public immersion in the name of Jesus Christ. From the word *saved* in this context, we learn that regeneration and belief go together. Those who "*believed* were together" and were designated as "*saved*" (Acts 2:44,47).

Clear Membership

No one partakes of the work of Christ through the standing of their parents or through baptism. There is no place for godparents. But in truth, no one partakes of the work of Christ through the standing of their parents or through baptism. There is no middle ground; either one is a believer and is saved or one is still lost and in sin. *Baptist polity clearly defines who is in and who is outside the church!*

Central to this Baptist perspective is that salvation fundamentally involves a *response* or choice on the part of the convert. Doctrinally, calling for a decision in a public invitation is logically connected in other Baptist beliefs such as soul responsibility and believer's baptism.

Not only does scriptural baptism remind the church of the gospel, and guard against theological liberalism, it also prevents the church from becoming a mere social institution. It reminds the church of the necessity of evangelism as the church's primary mission.

Believer's baptism keeps conversion as a priority, and it places a clear distinction between saved and lost (regenerate church membership).

Regenerate, Immersed Church Membership Makes Word-Centered Worship Possible

Baptists believe in Word-centered, local church instruction for all believers. Therefore, Baptist worship is not liturgical or sacramental but focuses on instruction and exhortation from the Bible. The early church was committed first to the teaching of the apostles (Acts 2:42). In fact, their desire for hearing and obeying the word of God through the Apostles was evidence of their regeneration (1 John 4:6) and resulted in clear requirements for membership and church life.

Where do we find the teaching of the apostles today? Our Lord brought to the memory of the apostles the things He taught and desired to be recorded. The Gospels were written from the firsthand experiences of the apostles. Jesus promised them, "But the Comforter… he shall teach you all things, and *bring all things to your remembrance*, whatsoever I have said unto you" (John 14:26). You can only remember what you have previously heard or known.

Jesus also led them into new understanding and to new revelation, which they wrote in order to give direction to the churches during this dispensation. He said, the Spirit of truth . . . *will guide you* into all truth . . . and he will shew you things to come (John 16:13). We need a guide when we are going into new territory. The epistles are the result of this promise, as the Holy Spirit guided the apostles in writing the inspired letters to the churches. The "things to come" that He would show them are the focus of the book of Revelation as well as other prophetic content in the teaching of our Lord.

Because the unregenerate cannot spiritually understand the teaching of the Scriptures (1 Cor. 2:14), regenerate, immersed membership makes the teaching of the Word of God effective, because the understanding of the Word is now possible for all members.

The order of the Great Commission, as commanded by the Lord Jesus, is evangelism, church association through baptism, and local church instruction. Regenerate, immersed church membership follows this command; and it both emphasizes and enables Word-centered worship as believers are instructed in all things the Lord has commanded.

Worship in Reformed churches tends to be liturgical. It employs repetition of a scripted liturgy—a fixed set of ceremonies and words which are used during public worship. Liturgy is designed for beauty and symbolism. The prescribed liturgical worship confers grace upon the participant. It tends to be mechanical, repetitious, and ornate; it employs clerical authority which subverts the priesthood of the believer; and it confers grace, often apart from intellectual understanding, to those who participate.

In contrast, the apostolic church continually gathered for Bible teaching; they were continuing steadfastly to hear and understand the teaching of the apostles. They sat under the preaching ministry of the apostles, whose teaching, now written on the pages of the New Testament Scriptures, is to be taught by all pastors.

Paul's letters to his protégés Timothy and Titus reflect both the priority of truth and of the preaching of the Word. God designed the church to be a place where His Word is proclaimed and explained. A commitment to the apostles' doctrine or teaching is foundational to the growth and spiritual health of every church. This is the heritage and the commitment of Baptist churches.

Regenerate, immersed church membership matters. It guards the gospel, protects the church, promotes evangelism and makes the teaching of the Word of God effective for all members. The Reformation brought a shift in public worship for many churches, from the centrality of the sacraments to the centrality of the reading and preaching of the Word. But it is the Baptists who have most consistently followed the Biblical pattern of the early church. Let us faithfully extend that commitment to the next generation.

Answers to Common Questions

The following are some common questions that I have been asked throughout my forty years of ministry. You will find more thorough information and argumentation in the text of this book, but succinct answers are given here for quick help.

What is baptism? Is the mode important?

To baptize means *to dip* or *immerse*. Immersion is important because only immersion illustrates the death, burial, and resurrection of Christ. Only immersion can picture the believer's death to the old life and resurrection to the new life in Christ.

What does baptism say about our conversion?

Conversion is an instantaneous, one-time event in the life of the believing sinner whereby he has died to his old life, is forgiven of his sins, and is raised to live a new life.

When should baptism take place?

Baptism is a testimony of one's faith in Christ. Therefore, it is improper to baptize someone incapable of the intellectual understanding necessary to exercise faith. Infants and very small children are unable to exercise biblical faith. It is also out of order to baptize any adult before they have experienced new life in Christ.

What is the relationship between baptism and the Lord's Supper?

Baptism pictures our one-time justification, whereas the repetition of the Lord's Supper observance reminds us of progressive sanctification. Upon baptism, the believer is united with the local church membership; whereas the Lord's Supper is celebrated when the church comes together, reminding us of the fellowship we have with the Lord and with one another.

Is baptism necessary for membership?

Yes, this is the pattern of the New Testament. The Lord Jesus' last command was to make disciples, to baptize them and to teach them to observe all that He has commanded. In this process, baptism comes before teaching. The teaching ministry of the local church is primarily directed toward the members of the local church.

Does an immersed believer need to be rebaptized to transfer church membership?

Believer's baptism is not normally repeated upon a believer's transfer to another local church. Since rebaptism violates the picture of a once-for-all time salvation, it may be as wrong to be rebaptized as it is to refuse or neglect baptism altogether.

It should not be required of anyone to be baptized again if he or she had been immersed after confession of faith in Christ. This would be true in all cases except when the baptism was received through a church which perverts the gospel.

Is membership necessary for partaking in the Lord's Supper?

The Lord's Supper logically and theologically follows baptism in the same way as sanctification follows justification. If the Lord's Supper follows baptism, and baptism is a prerequisite to church membership, then church membership is a requirement for participation in the Lord's Supper. To say it another way, one must begin the Christian life before one may continue; one must enter the church relationship before one is able to continue in fellowship.

May pedobaptists be included in the celebration of the Supper?

Those who have never been scripturally baptized should not participate in the Lord's Supper. Sprinkling is not baptism because

146

baptism is immersion. Those who are baptized—using any mode—as infants were not believers at the time and therefore their baptism would be invalid.

Does baptism require church membership?

This is the opposite of the former question. Not only is baptism a requirement for church membership, but baptism requires church membership. Baptism not only symbolizes the believer's new life in Christ (Rom 6:1-3), it also symbolizes the beginning of the believer's church relationship (1 Cor 12:13). Upon believing in Christ, the sinner is forgiven and instantaneously baptized by the Holy Spirit and placed into the body of Christ. Water baptism and local church membership picture this reality. No one ought to be baptized who is unwilling to publicly identify with the church. An unwillingness to identify with the Lord's body, of which He is the head, and His building project, which is where He is working in this age, is a concerning sign.

What does the Lord's Supper teach concerning sanctification?

The fact that the Lord's Supper is celebrated often teaches that there is no sinless perfection in this life. The Lord's Supper is practiced until Jesus comes and all church-age believers experience final, complete sanctification. At that time, our faith will be sight and we will no longer struggle with sin.

Are the elements important?

The unleavened bread represents our Lord's sinless life and the cup containing the fruit of the vine pictures His blood shed for us. These elements of the Lord's Supper signify our life of faithful dependence in partaking of the bread and our need for continual cleansing in the drinking of the cup.

At what age should a believer be baptized?

The one being baptized must be mature enough to make an

autonomous, personal decision. This doesn't mean that they must have a comprehensive understanding of Bible doctrine. However, they must have a basic understanding of sin, its consequences, and its remedy in Jesus Christ. To grasp this remedy, a person must have a clear, though surely not complete, knowledge of the person and work of Christ. Jesus is both God and perfect man, who died to take the sinner's punishment. He was raised and is alive.

Verifiable conversion, as seen in its results, is a qualification for candidates of all ages as well. Many have noted the obvious work of God's Spirit in children as young as three and four years old, observing in them a brand new desire for truthfulness and obedience. It is not unusual for the same young children to then be concerned for the souls of unsaved siblings and friends.

Baptism should not be imposed upon children or anyone. It ought to be performed by request of the candidate.

My child does not understand baptism. Can my child participate in communion even though they are not baptized?

If a child is too young to understand baptism, then they are too young to understand the meaning of the Lord's Supper. Sanctification is at least as complex as the doctrine of justification. A child can believe and be saved but not without an understanding of the basics of the gospel. Like any adult believer, a child must begin the Christian life before they can continue; baptism comes before the Lord's Supper.

I don't feel worthy. Should I participate if I am struggling with sin?

If perfection was the standard, then no one could partake of the Supper. Surely, there is an implicit acknowledgement in taking the cup that we are not without sin. We are all forgiven sinners and we will continue to struggle against sin until we are glorified in the presence of Christ.

There is a difference between struggling with a besetting sin and refusing to deal with sin. When one's heart is set against the will of God, the believer is in a spiritually dangerous place. Repentance is the need. The Lord's Supper pictures our ongoing fellowship with Christ, and there can be no fellowship until sin is confessed.

Bibliography

Armitage, Thomas. *A History of the Baptists*. Watertown, WI: Roger Williams Heritage Archives, 1886.

Bacon, Leonard Woolsey. *A History of American Christianity*. New York: The Christian Literature Co., 1897.

Baker, Robert A., and John M. Landers. *A Summary of Christian History, 3rd edition*. Nashville, TN: Broadman & Holman Publishers, 2005. eBook.

Bahnsen, Greg. The Concept and Importance of Canonicity. http://www.reformed.org/master /index.html?mainframe=/bible/bahnsen_canon. html.

Baptist News Global. "Baptism Meanings and Methods Spark Debate among Some Baptists," June 22, 2006. https://baptistnews.com/article/baptism-meanings-and-methods-spark-debate-among-some-baptists/#.XQkMdYhKhPY.

Bonchie. "Democrats Go to War with the Catholic Church." RedState.com, June 18, 2021. https://redstate.com/bonchie/2021/06/18/demo crats-go-to-war-with-the-catholic-church-n398957.

Brand, Edward P. *Illinois Baptists: A History*. Bloomington, IL: Pantagraph Printing Company, 1930.

Calvin, John. *Institutes of the Christian Religion.*
Bellingham: WA: Logos Bible Software, 1997.

Colby, Henry Francis. *Restriction of the Lord's Supper.*
Watertown, WI: Roger Williams Heritage
Archives, 1853.

Criswell, Dr. W. A. "The Ordinances of the Church." W.A.
Criswell Sermon Library. Accessed December 9,
2023. https:// wacriswell.com/sermons/1982
/the-ordinances-of-the-church1/.

Cummins, David L., and E. Wayne Thompson. This Day in
Baptist History: 366 Daily Devotions Drawn from
the Baptist Heritage. Greenville, SC: BJU Press,
1993.

Cummins, David L., and E. Wayne Thompson. *This Day in
Baptist History II: 366 Daily Devotions.* Greenville,
SC: BJU Press, 2000.

Cummins, David L. *This Day in Baptist History III. David
Cummins, 2006.*

Curnock, Nehemiah, ed. *The Journal of John Wesley,
Volume 1.* London: Epworth Press, 1938.

Elwell, Walter A., ed. *Baker Encyclopedia of the Bible.*
Grand Rapids, MI: Baker Book House, 1988.
Logos Bible Software.

Feddes, David. "Should Babies Be Baptized?" Accessed
January 10, 2024.

https://www.crcna.org/welcome/beliefs/positio-
statements /baptism/should-babies-be-baptized.

Galbreath, Paul. "Sacraments: Grace We Can Touch."
    Presbyterians Today, June 2014. First published
    2009. https://www.presbyterianmission.org
    /what-we-believe/sacraments/.

Garland, David E. *First Corinthians*. Grand Rapids, MI.:
    Baker Academic, 2003.

Gear, H. L. *The Relation of Baptism to the Lord's Supper*.
    Watertown, WI: Roger Williams Heritage
    Archives, 1880; 2003.

Gordon, T. David. Why Johnny Can't Preach: The Media
    Have Shaped the Messengers. Phillipsburg, N.J:
    P&R Publishing, 2009.

Hamilton, Jr., James M. "The Lord's Supper in Paul: An
    Identity-Forming Proclamation of the Gospel,"
    2010. https:// jimhamilton.info/wp-
    content/uploads/2010/12/lords-supper-in-paul-
    formtted.pdf.

Hay, Alex Rattray. *The New Testament Order for Church
    and Missionary*. Eugene, OR: Wipf and Stock
    Publishers, 2010.

Hayden, Eric. "Johann Gerhard Oncken: Friend of
    Spurgeon." Banner of Truth USA, September 22,
    2017. https://banneroftruth.org/us
    /resources/articles/2017/johann-gerhard-
    oncken-friend-spurgeon/.

Heine, Ronald E. Classical Christian Doctrine: *Introducing the Essentials of the Ancient Faith*. Grand Rapids, MI: Baker Academic, 2013.

Hening, William Waller. The Statutes at Large: Being a Collection of All the Laws of Virginia, from the First Session of the Legislature, in the Year 1619, Volume IX. Richmond, VA: Printed for the editor, by J & G. Cochran, Printers, 1821. 1969 facsimile. https://vagenweb.org/hening/.

Hiscox, Edward Thurston. *The New Directory for Baptist Churches, 1962 Edition*. Valley Forge: The Judson Press, 1894.

Hoeksema, Herman. *Reformed Dogmatics*. Jenison, MI: Reformed Free Publishing Association, 1966.

Marshall, Ian Howard. "The Meaning of the Verb 'to baptize,'" *Evangelical Quarterly: An International Review of Bible and Theology,* 45, 3, 1973.

Hunt, Dave. What Love Is This? Calvinism's Misrepresentation of God. Bend, OR: Berean Call, 2007.

Jackson, Paul Rainey. *The Doctrine and Administration of the Church*. Des Plaines, IL: Regular Baptist Press, 1968.

Jamieson, Bobby. *Going Public: Why Baptism Is Required for Church Membership*. Nashville, TN: B&H Academic 2015. EBSCO Publishing: eBook Collection.

Lemke, Steve. "What Is A Baptist? Nine Marks that Separate Baptists from Presbyterians." *Journal for Baptist Theology & Ministry*, Fall 2008.

Letham, Robert W. A. The Westminster Assembly: Reading Its Theology in Historical Context. Phillipsburg, NJ: P & R Pub, 2009.

Little, Lewis Peyton. *Imprisoned Preachers and Religious Liberty in Virginia*. Lynchburg, VA: J. P. Bell Company, Inc., 1938.

Luther, Martin. Leupold, Ulrich S., ed. *Luther's Works, Volume 53: Liturgy and Hymns*. Philadelphia: Fortress Press, 1965.

Luther, Martin. *Three Treatises*. Philadelphia: Fortress Press, 1970.

Morell, Caleb. "How Harry Emerson Fosdick's 'Open Membership' Overtook the Northern Baptist Convention." 9Marks, August 1, 2022. https://www.9marks.org/article/how-harry-emerson-fosdicks-open-membership-overtook-the-northern-baptist-convention/.

Muir, William. *Our Grand Old Bible*. London: Morgan and Scott, 1911.

Otto, Joel D. "Alive in Christ: An Exegetical Study of Colossians 2:6–15," Wisconsin Lutheran Seminary Essay File, 2010. Accessed January 11, 2024. http://essays.wisluthsem.org:8080/handle/123456789/3545.

Pettingill, William Leroy. *The Evils of Infant Baptism*. St. Paul, MN: Northland Publishing, 1947.

Placher, William C. Readings in the History of Christian Theology, Volume 2: From the Reformation to the Present. Philadelphia, PA: The Westminster Press, 1988.

Richards, George W. *The Heidelberg Catechism: Historical and Doctrinal Studies*. Philadelphia: Publication and Sunday School Board of the Reformed Church in the United States, 1913.

Saxon, David. "The Logic of BRAPSIS." Maranatha Baptist University, September 1, 2006. https://www.mbu.edu/seminary/the-logic-of-brapsis/.

Schaff, Philip, and Schaff, David Schley. *History of the Christian Church, Volume 1*, Apostolic Christianity A. D. 1-100, 3rd Edition. New York: Charles Scribner's Sons, 1907.

Spurgeon, Charles. *Spurgeon's Sermons Volume XIII: The Metropolitan Tabernacle Pulpit*, 1867. https://archive.org/details/SpurgeonMetropolitanPt13/page/n713/mode/2up.

Spurgeon, Charles. "Truly Eating the Flesh of Jesus." Sermon No. 1288, delivered April 9, 1876, Metropolitan Tabernacle Pulpit, Newington (London). https:// www.spurgeongems.org/ sermon/chs1288.pdf.

Spurgeon, Charles. "Fencing the Table." Sermon No. 2865, delivered January 2, 1876, Metropolitan Tabernacle Pulpit, Newington (London). https://biblebb.com/files/spurgeon/2865.htm.

Spurgeon, Charles. "The Right Observance of the Lord's Supper." Sermon No. 2638, delivered June 4, 1882, The Metropolitan Tabernacle Pulpit, Newington (London). https://www.spurgeongems.org/sermon/chs2638.pdf.

Spurgeon, Charles. "Signs of the Times." Sermon No. 1135, delivered October 5, 1873, Metropolitan Tabernacle Pulpit, Newington (London). https://www.spurgeongems.org/sermon/chs1135.pdf.

Stuart, Moses. Is the Mode of Christian Baptism Prescribed in the New Testament? Nashville: Graves, Mark & Rutland, 1855.

Underwood, A. C., and J. H. Rushbrooke. *A History of the English Baptists*. London: The Baptist Union Publications, 1947. Quoted in Johannes Warns, *Baptism*.

Ursinus, Zacharius, et al. *Heidelberg Catechism*. Translated by the Reformed Church, 1978. Heidelberg, Germany: University of Heidelberg, 1563. Accessed January 10, 2024. https://heidelblog.net/catechism/.

Warns, Johannes. *Baptism*. Translated by G. H. Lang. London: The Paternoster Press, 1957.

Wayland, Francis. A Memoir of the Life and Labors of the Rev. Adoniram Judson, D.D., Vol. I. Boston: Phillips, Sampson, and Company, 1853. Quoted in Dr. David Cummins, This Day in Baptist History Volume One.

Wesley, John, and Nehemiah Curnock, Ed. *The Journal of John Wesley, Volume 1*. London: The Epworth Press, 1938.

Westminster Confession of Faith 1646, XXVIII.I.

White, James. *The Potter's Freedom*. Amityville, NY: Calvary Press Publishing, 2000.